Cite-Checker

Third Edition

ASPEN COLLEGE SERIES

Cite-Checker
Your Guide to Using
The Bluebook

Third Edition

Deborah E. Bouchoux, Esq.
Georgetown University

Wolters Kluwer
Law & Business

AUSTIN   BOSTON   CHICAGO   NEW YORK   THE NETHERLANDS

Aspen Publishers
Attn: Permissions Department
76 Ninth Avenue, 7th Floor
New York, NY 10011-5201

To contact Customer Care, e-mail customer.service@aspenpublishers.com,
call 1-800-234-1660, fax 1-800-901-9075, or mail correspondence to:

Aspen Publishers
Attn: Order Department
PO Box 990
Frederick, MD 21705

Printed in the United States of America.

1 2 3 4 5 6 7 8 9 0

ISBN 978-0-7355-8766-3

Library of Congress Cataloging-in-Publication Data

Bouchoux, Deborah E., 1950-
Cite-Checker : your guide to using the bluebook/Deborah E.
Bouchoux. — 3rd ed.
    p. cm. — (Aspen College Series)
  Includes bibliographical references and index.
  ISBN 978-0-7355-8766-3 (alk. paper)
  1. Citation of legal authorities — United States. I. Title.
KF245.B68 2011
340.01'48 — dc22

2010046342

About Wolters Kluwer Law & Business

Wolters Kluwer Law & Business is a leading provider of research information and workflow solutions in key specialty areas. The strength of the individual brands of Aspen Publishers, CCH, Kluwer Law International and Loislaw are aligned within Wolters Kluwer Law & Business to provide comprehensive, in-depth solutions and expert-authored content for the legal, professional and education markets.

CCH was founded in 1913 and has served more than four generations of business professionals and their clients. The CCH products in the Wolters Kluwer Law & Business group are highly regarded electronic and print resources for legal, securities, antitrust and trade regulation, government contracting, banking, pension, payroll, employment and labor, and health-care reimbursement and compliance professionals.

Aspen Publishers is a leading information provider for attorneys, business professionals and law students. Written by preeminent authorities, Aspen products offer analytical and practical information in a range of specialty practice areas from securities law and intellectual property to mergers and acquisitions and pension/benefits. Aspen's trusted legal education resources provide professors and students with high-quality, up-to-date and effective resources for successful instruction and study in all areas of the law.

Kluwer Law International supplies the global business community with comprehensive English-language international legal information. Legal practitioners, corporate counsel and business executives around the world rely on the Kluwer Law International journals, loose-leafs, books and electronic products for authoritative information in many areas of international legal practice.

Loislaw is a premier provider of digitized legal content to small law firm practitioners of various specializations. Loislaw provides attorneys with the ability to quickly and efficiently find the necessary legal information they need, when and where they need it, by facilitating access to primary law as well as state-specific law, records, forms and treatises.

Wolters Kluwer Law & Business, a unit of Wolters Kluwer, is headquartered in New York and Riverwoods, Illinois. Wolters Kluwer is a leading multinational publisher and information services company.

Dedication

*For my husband, Donald, and our children
Meaghan, Elizabeth, Patrick, and Robert*

Contents

Preface

The task of checking one's own citations or those of another author to ensure they comply with the format of *The Bluebook: A Uniform System of Citation* (Columbia Law Review Ass'n et al. eds., 19th ed. 2010) is usually called cite-checking or "Bluebooking." *The Bluebook* consists of more than 400 pages of rules and tables. Some of these rules are poorly explained and others are inconsistent and arbitrary. For example, when sending a reader to a page within an immediately preceding authority, one uses the form "*id.* at 16." However, when sending the reader to a paragraph or section within an immediately preceding authority, one uses "*id.* § 16" or "*id.* ¶ 16." In other words, one cannot use the word "at" before a section symbol or paragraph sign. Why? No one knows. Similarly, one must place a comma after the title of a law review article or annotation but not after a book title. These and myriad other inconsistencies make cite-checking a frustrating task for nearly all legal writers.

For practitioners, the task is complicated even further by the fact that *The Bluebook* is designed for use by law students or those writing academic law review or law journal articles. Most of the examples given in *The Bluebook* are presented in a particular style of typeface, called "large and small capitals," that practitioners do not use. Moreover, full case names throughout nearly all of *The Bluebook* are neither underscored nor italicized, whereas practitioners always underscore or italicize case names.

In sum, practitioners have lacked a clear and brief guide to citation form designed exclusively for them. After years of teaching legal research and providing numerous in-house seminars for practitioners at law firms, government agencies, and in-house legal departments, it became clear to me that practitioners were woefully underserved by *The Bluebook*. It is my hope that this book fills the need for a short and simple guide to the most common types of citations used by practitioners so that the task of cite-checking will be easier and less frustrating.

■ Use of This Book

All legal authorities can be categorized into one of two broad categories: primary authorities and secondary authorities. Primary authorities include cases, statutes, constitutions, and administrative regulations (such as regulations of the Food and Drug Administration [FDA] or Federal Communications Commission [FCC]). Nearly everything else (including books, articles, and law dictionaries) is a secondary authority. Legal writers typically prefer to cite primary authorities rather than secondary authorities because courts are bound to follow primary authorities from their jurisdiction, assuming these authorities are relevant or "on point." Primary authorities are thus usually referred to as "binding" or "mandatory," whereas secondary authorities are described as "persuasive."

This book is arranged in a building-block approach. First, users should master primary authorities, namely, the most frequently cited authorities: cases and statutes. They will then be ready to move on to secondary authorities and then to the use of quotations, signals, and short forms. In each instance, *The Bluebook* rules are explained, and then examples (most of which are fictitious) are given.

For the most thorough mastery of citation form, users should start at Chapter 1 and continue reading through the text, doing the pertinent exercises along the way. An answer key for each exercise is printed at the back of this book. Although users will quickly be able to memorize some citation forms, most legal writers continually refer to *The Bluebook* to ensure a citation is correct. No one expects legal writers to have mastered all of *The Bluebook* rules together with their numerous exceptions. Thus, continual reference to *The Bluebook* while preparing answers to the exercises herein and while on the job is expected.

As new topics are introduced throughout this book, references are given to the guiding rules or sections in *The Bluebook*. Thus, a reference to "Rule 15" refers to Rule 15 in *The Bluebook*, and a reference to "B9" refers to Bluepages Rule 9 of *The Bluebook*. References to tables, such as Table T.1, refer to tables in *The Bluebook*.

When dates in sample citations are shown as "(19xx)," acceptable formats include dates from other centuries if appropriate.

■ Scope of This Book

This guide covers most of the basic citation rules, giving several examples. It is impossible, however, to give complete coverage to *Bluebook* rules without nearly duplicating the size of the original *Bluebook*. Moreover, there are authorities that even *The Bluebook* does not address. When confronted with such material, *The Bluebook* suggests that one try to locate an analogous authority, always guided by the principle that a writer must ensure a reader can find the cited authority quickly and reliably.

Although putting citations into their proper form is the hardest component of cite-checking, there is one other component to the task: "Shepardizing" (if using print volumes or the LexisNexis computer research system) or "KeyCiting" (if using the Westlaw computer research system), which are methods to ensure authorities cited are still good law. This book does not cover Shepardizing or KeyCiting. It is designed solely for the purpose of assisting legal writers in proper citation form. For information on Shepardizing or KeyCiting (which are now done electronically rather than through the use of print volumes in nearly every law firm and legal department), consult textbooks on legal research or access LexisNexis's website at http:// w3.lexis.com/lawschoolreg/tutorials/shepards and use the tutorial to learn how to Shepardize. Alternatively, access Westlaw's site at http://west. thomson.com/support/user-guide/keycite.aspx for West's User Guide to KeyCiting and other product information. Finally, most of the examples in this book are fictitious.

Please note that Internet resources are of a time-sensitive nature and URL addresses can often change or be deleted.

Acknowledgments

No publication is the product solely of its author. Many individuals contributed significantly to the development of this guide to citation form. As always, my first thoughts and gratitude go to Susan M. Sullivan, Director of the Paralegal Program at the University of San Diego, who provided me with my first teaching opportunity. Sue is a valued colleague and a dear friend.

Special thanks to my many students who, with their probing questions and curiosity, prompted me to continue trying to master the intricacies of *The Bluebook*. The reviewers who evaluated the original manuscript of this publication provided prompt and clear analysis and must, therefore, be recognized:

Ms. Suzanne Bailey, Western Illinois University
Mr. Adam Epstein, University of Tennessee
Mr. John Frank, Chippewa Valley Technical College
Mr. Chris Whaley, Roane State Community College
Ms. Donna Bookin, Mercy College
Ms. Julia O. Tryk, Cuyahoga Community College
Ms. Patricia Adongo, University of LaVerne
Ms. Barbara Ricker, Andover College

I would like to express my most sincere appreciation to the following individuals at Aspen Publishers who provided continued encouragement and support throughout the development of *Cite-Checker*: David Herzig, Associate Publisher, College Market; Betsy Kenny, Development Editor; Kaesmene Harrison Banks, Senior Editor; Teresa Horton, copy editor; and Rosalie Briand, proofreader.

Finally, deepest thanks and love to my husband Don and our children Meaghan, Elizabeth, Patrick, and Robert, for their unflagging patience and understanding while I continually pored over *The Bluebook* while writing this guide to citation form.

I would also like to thank West, a Thomson Reuters business, for its permission to reprint Figure 3-4, the map of the thirteen federal judicial circuits, that appears in Chapter 3 and is reprinted in the Federal Reporter.

1

Introduction to Cite-Checking

The Task of Cite-Checking

A 500-plus page book entitled *The Bluebook: A Uniform System of Citation* (Columbia Law Review Ass'n et al. eds., 19th ed. 2010) (*The Bluebook*) is the standard reference tool in the United States for citing legal authorities. Although some states, including California, Michigan, and Texas, have their own citation systems and manuals and many courts have established rules governing citation for documents submitted to them, *The Bluebook* remains the gold standard for citation form throughout the United States, primarily because the judges who read court briefs learned *Bluebook* citation form when in school.

The principle underlying *The Bluebook* is that citation form for cases, statutes, and other authorities should be consistent throughout the entire United States, so that a practitioner in Ohio can submit a brief to a New York court, and all readers will know how and where to locate the authorities referred to in the document. The task of placing citations in their proper format is typically called "cite-checking" or "Bluebooking."

Why must a practitioner learn the intricate and difficult rules of citation form? First, citation form communicates critical information to a reader because it allows a reader to locate and review authorities referred to in a legal document. Thus, an organized, systematic, uniform system of citation is needed so all law practitioners cite cases, statutes, and other authorities the same way each time they are used. Second, although incorrect citation form is not an act of legal malpractice, it reflects badly on you and your firm or company, much the same way a spelling error has a disproportionately negative effect on a reader. Carelessness in citation form could lead a reader to believe you are equally careless in your analysis of the law. Law firms and departments strive for excellence and professionalism to best serve their clients. Correct citation form is an integral part of this goal. Nevertheless, there is tremendous inconsistency in citation form often contributed to by courts themselves, which frequently use incorrect citation form in their own published opinions. Similarly, law book publishers contribute to misunderstanding of citation form by often using incorrect citation form, typically in an effort to save space and reduce printing costs.

Recently, courts have been complaining that too many briefs are riddled with citation errors. *See, e.g., Edison Mission Energy, Inc. v. FERC*, 394 F.3d 964, 969 n.1 (D.C. Cir. 2005) (noting that failure to indicate relevant pages in citations in briefs is sanctionable under the Federal Rules of Appellate Procedure).

Practice Tip

✓ Do not rely on citation form used in published case reports or other legal authorities, including Lexis and Westlaw. To save space or to emphasize market brand, these forms are often incorrect. Use *The Bluebook*.

■ *The Bluebook*

Introduction

The Bluebook is the accepted "bible" for citation form (unless court rules dictate otherwise). Yet its myriad rules are awkwardly phrased, haphazardly arranged, and seemingly contradictory. Why? *The Bluebook* was originally intended as a short guide to aid law students in preparing citations in their scholarly writings. Eventually, as legal authorities proliferated, so did the rules in *The Bluebook*. Additionally, it began to be accepted as the citation form authority for practitioners as well as for those engaged in scholarly writing, although the presentation style used for academic writing (a style that used LARGE AND SMALL CAPITALS) could not be reproduced by practitioners who were typing their documents rather than having them professionally typeset. Thus, one citation guide attempts to fit vastly differing needs.

Moreover, *The Bluebook's* coverage might simply be too broad. In providing information about citing to Swiss civil law cases, Belgian treaties, and Zambian statutes, little space is available to provide examples of far less esoteric citation forms, such as those for New York cases.

Thus, *The Bluebook's* numerous rules and their exceptions, dual approach, and broad coverage have contributed to frustration for cite-checkers. Moreover, cite-checking is often done at the eleventh hour, making it a difficult and pressure-filled task. Finally, it requires attention to detail and a high level of concentration to locate minute errors in spacing and abbreviations. All of these factors contribute to an often difficult task. By learning the most frequently used citation rules, however, in a step-by-step approach, you will achieve mastery of this task.

Although there are other citation guides, such as *The Maroonbook* (published by the University of Chicago Law Review and used primarily in the Chicago metropolitan area), or *ALWD*, a user-friendly citation manual published by the Association of Legal Writing Directors and Professor Darby Dickerson (now in its fourth edition), *The Bluebook* is the most widely adopted system of citation in practice and should be followed unless court rules or law firm or company policy require otherwise.

History of *The Bluebook*

The Bluebook is compiled by the editors of the *Columbia Law Review, Harvard Law Review, University of Pennsylvania Law Review,* and *The Yale Law Journal.* Originally compiled in the mid-1920s, *The Bluebook* was a small pamphlet designed to instruct scholarly writers and the printers of scholarly articles in citation form. Over the years, *The Bluebook* was revised a number of times. The present edition in use is the Nineteenth Edition. Earlier editions have little, if any, practical value and can be discarded. New editions are not released at regularly scheduled intervals but rather when the editors believe changes are needed. The Nineteenth Edition was issued in mid-2010 and includes a number of new features, including changes dictated by new technologies (such as allowing increased citation to Internet sources).

Changes in *The Bluebook* over time can result in some citations being incorrect now that might have been correct several years ago when they were first prepared. Thus, exercise care when importing citations from a previously written document into your document. Ensure citations you use conform to present-day *Bluebook* rules.

Organization of *The Bluebook*

Spend a few minutes becoming familiar with the organization of *The Bluebook*. In particular, note the following:

- Examine the Preface to the Nineteenth Edition (pages vii and viii). These pages outline changes made in the Nineteenth Edition of *The Bluebook*. When the next edition of *The Bluebook* is issued, examine this section to learn new rules and changes.
- Review the section on light blue paper beginning on page 3, called "the Bluepages." The examples found on pages 3-27 are ready for use by practitioners, meaning there is no need to convert typeface or make other changes to adapt *Bluebook* forms, originally intended for scholarly writers, for use in the "real world." The Bluepages show how to adapt the examples found in the body of *The Bluebook* to the format needed for court documents and legal memoranda. The Bluepages are far more complete and extensive than the prior Practitioners' Notes (found in the Seventeenth Edition) and provide numerous helpful examples.
- Note Table T.1. After setting forth rules about federal court cases, there is a thorough section devoted to federal administrative and executive materials and then a section devoted to citation form for the states, each of which is listed in alphabetical order. A reference is provided for each state's judicial website. Although you will not be given examples, you will be provided with a blueprint for setting up citations for the cases and statutes in each state.
- Table T.10 provides abbreviations for each state. Note that the abbreviations might not conform to your expectation as to how to abbreviate a particular state's name. Similarly, Table T.12 provides abbreviations for the months of the year. These are but two examples of *The Bluebook*'s insistence on uniformity.
- All of the Tables at the back of *The Bluebook* are banded in blue, making it easy for you to access these important resources.
- The Index, printed on white paper at the end of *The Bluebook*, provides a ready reference to locating information. It is well-organized and complete.
- The outside back cover provides a mini-Index to *The Bluebook*, making it easy to find various rules.

Practice Tip

✓ Because there are parts of *The Bluebook* that you might not use (for example, Tables T.2, T.3, T.4, and T.5, the tables relating to international materials), simply clip them closed with a binder clip, so they don't slow you down as you search for information in your *Bluebook*.

New Features of the Nineteenth Edition of *The Bluebook*

The new Nineteenth Edition of *The Bluebook* provides a number of new features, including the following:

- **Bluepages.** The Bluepages section (which was new to the Eighteenth Edition) has been expanded. For example, it now includes information on citing to Electronic Case Filings.
- **Bluepages Table T.2.** Bluepages Table T.2 (providing references to local rules that govern citation form) has been expanded.
- **Order of parentheticals.** *Bluebook* Rule 1.5 now provides an order or ranking for parentheticals when a writer uses several of them.
- **Administrative materials.** Much of the information that was previously included in Rule 14 (covering Administrative and Executive Materials) is now in Table T.1.2. Moreover, Table T.1.2 (see page 218) now gives an expanded list of federal agencies, including information on citing to materials from NOAA, the USPTO, Department of Homeland Security, and more.
- **Electronic and Internet sources.** Rule 18, relating to citation to electronic sources (namely, the Internet, Lexis, and Westlaw) has been revised, and citation to these electronic sources is simplified, although *The Bluebook* continues to require the use and citation of traditional printed sources when they are available *unless* there is a digital copy of the source available that is authenticated, official, or an exact copy of the printed source (in which case the authenticated, official, or exact copy can be cited as if to the original print source).
- **Table T.1.** Table T.1 has now been divided into four sections: federal judicial and legislative materials; federal administrative and executive materials; states; and other U.S. jurisdictions.

Practice Tip

> ✓ Make *The Bluebook* work for you. Use sticky flags to tab the sections you rely on most frequently, such as the Bluepages, Rule 10 (relating to cases), Rule 12 (relating to statutes), Table T.1 (providing rules for citing cases and statutes in all U.S. jurisdictions), Table T.6 (providing abbreviations), and the Index (allowing you easy access to the rules you need).

Top Ten Tips for Effective Cite-Checking

Because cite-checking is typically an eleventh-hour assignment and requires painstaking attention to detail, the task requires patience and a highly organized approach. The following tips will make your task more manageable.

1. **Highlight all citations.** Your first step should be to take a colored marker and highlight all citations (both primary and secondary authorities) in a document. You might be surprised to discover that after an hour or so, the citations tend to blend into the text of the document, particularly when italics are used rather than underscoring. Thus, if you highlight each citation when you are fresh, you will readily be able to locate and check each citation when your attention might be flagging. Consider using a pink highlighter to mark all cases, blue for statutes, and so forth. A color-coded system will allow you to check all authorities of the same type at once, which could be easier than switching back and forth between different types of authorities.

2. **Get instructions.** If cite-checking for another, ask the author or the supervisor who assigned the cite-checking assignment whether you can assume numbers and dates are correct and that you, therefore, need only check spacing, punctuation, and other format considerations, or whether you should do a "top to bottom" check and verify the accuracy of every number and date. When in doubt, err on the side of caution, and do the most thorough check possible. Similarly, ask if the author or the judge to whom the document is being

sent has a preference for underscoring rather than italicizing case names and book titles. This will save time later if your first draft uses italics, and the author or judge insists all case names and book titles be underscored.

3. **Ask for help.** If cite-checking for another writer, call or e-mail your colleagues and ask if anyone has done a cite-checking assignment for that particular author and whether the author has any particular preferences or quirks. Similarly, if the document is addressed to a court, ask if anyone has recently filed a document with that court. Using a model will give you a certain comfort level. Save your cite-checked briefs, and make your own model form files.

4. **Know the rules.** Many courts have mandated their own rules for citation form. For example, California Rule of Court 1.200 provides that citations in court documents must conform to the *California Style Manual* or *The Bluebook*. If your document is addressed to a court, determine if such rules exist. If they do, they supersede *The Bluebook* rules. To determine whether court rules exist, ask your law librarian (if your firm has one) to call the clerk of the court and inquire, or check the Internet. For home pages of all federal courts, access http://www.uscourts.gov, and follow the instructions to locate rules of court. For state court rules, access http://www.megalaw.com and select "State Law." You can then select the desired state and link directly to its rules of court. Remember to review Table BT.2 in *The Bluebook*, which provides references to local rules that relate to citation form. Also, check Table T.1 of *The Bluebook*, which identifies judicial websites for each state. Similarly, some law firms and law departments have their own practices and procedures for citation form. Ask if such policies exist.

5. **Support your corrections.** As you correct citations in the document, write legibly so the individual who later word processes the document can readily make the appropriate corrections. Note on your draft the page of *The Bluebook* or the pertinent rule that supports your correction. For example, if the author has used a broken line for the subsequent history signal rev'd en banc and your review of page 13 of *The Bluebook* shows it as rev'd en banc, jot "page 13" near your correction. If the author later challenges your correction, you will be prepared to show support for your work. What should you do if an author ignores your correct work and insists on using

an incorrect form? Give in. The person who signs the document should have the final decision on its contents.

6. **Develop a system.** As you make corrections, use a code or system to remind yourself which citations have been checked and which remain to be corrected. Use checks, asterisks, colored pens, colored adhesive flags, or any other method that works for you. Then if your work is interrupted and you later need to return to the project, you can readily determine where you need to start.

7. **Work smart.** As you correct citations, you will undoubtedly notice that there are "holes" in the document, such as missing dates or missing pages of quotes. Rather than immediately filling in each gap as you come across it, mark each gap with a colored highlighter or adhesive flag. Later, you can either go to the law library or go online and locate all of the missing information in one efficient step rather than attempting a piecemeal approach. Use Lexis or Westlaw to help you verify the accuracy of case names, pages, quotations, dates, and so forth. Similarly, if cite-checking for another, ask if the person has copies of the cases and other authorities cited in the brief. If so, sections of the cases might already be highlighted, allowing you to easily check the accuracy of quotations and other items.

8. **Be thorough.** Check all citations in the document. Ignore the temptation to focus on the argument section of a brief. Start at page one and look for every citation in the document, including those in the table of authorities, in footnotes, and any citations in any appendices.

9. **Be consistent.** If the author has been underscoring case names, ensure that book titles and citation signals such as id. and supra are likewise underscored. Conversely, if case names have been italicized, italicize book titles and signals

10. **Check the signals.** Citation signals such as *id.* tell a reader that a previously given citation supports a later statement. If you see signals such as *id.* and *supra*, check to ensure they match up with a previous citation. Why would they not? On many occasions an author might omit, insert, or move a section of a brief, forgetting that following signals could then be left hanging without a previous reference.

Practice Tips

✓ To ensure quick access to court rules, use the Internet site MegaLaw (http://www.megalaw.com), and bookmark the sites for the courts to which your office or firm routinely submits documents.

✓ Use standard proofreaders' marks when making corrections on a document. Some of the most frequently used marks are as follows:

#	Insert a space
⌒	Close up
∧	Insert
stet	Let the original text stand
ϒ	Delete text

✓ Images and examples of proofreaders' marks can be found at the following website: http://www.utexas.edu/visualguidelines/proofreaders.html.

Practice Tips

✓ Professor Peter W. Martin of Cornell University Law School has published an online guide to citation form entitled *Introduction to Basic Legal Citation* (rev. 2010). The guide provides information on the purpose of legal citations, examples for nearly all citation formats, and a table of state-specific citations, providing examples for cases, statutes, and regulations for all 50 states and the District of Columbia.

✓ The website address is http://www.law.cornell.edu/citation.

✓ Consider "bookmarking" this valuable site as one of your favorite sites. Use it as a "backup" or to confirm the accuracy of your citations.

✓ Caveat: Although this site is excellent and provides great examples, always use *The Bluebook* as the final authority. Nevertheless, this website will provide you with a wealth of valuable information and numerous examples of citation form.

2 The Bluebook Trap: Typeface Conventions

Guiding Principle: Practitioners should be wary of most of the examples given in The Bluebook *other than those in the Bluepages (pages 3-27). Although the words in the examples are in the right order and the spacing and punctuation are correct, the presentation style is inappropriate for practitioners in that large and small capitals are used. According to* The Bluebook, *practitioners do not use large and small capitals and must convert any large and small capital styles to ordinary roman typeface.*

▩ The Problem

Examine the inside front cover of *The Bluebook*, left side, approximately halfway down the page. Note the reference to the following state constitution:

N.M. Const. art. IV, § 7.

Now examine the inside back cover of *The Bluebook* in the same location. Examine the reference to the same constitution:

N.M. Const. art. IV, § 7.

Can you tell the difference in the style in which the same source is presented?

Note that in the first example, the capital letters "N," "M," and the "C" in "Const." are all slightly larger than the remaining capital letters in the word "Const." whereas in the second example from the inside back cover the presentation shows only an initial capital letter.

What is going on? How can both be correct? Return to your copy of *The Bluebook*. Note the heading on the inside front cover: Quick Reference: Law Review Footnotes. Compare this with the heading on the inside back cover: Quick Reference: Court Documents and Legal Memoranda.

You are now ready to tackle perhaps the single most confusing thing about *The Bluebook*. Nearly all of the examples given in its white pages are for use in law review footnotes and academic writing rather than for use by practitioners.

The Bluebook Approach

The Bluebook was originally developed solely for citations appearing in scholarly and academic articles appearing in law school publications, namely law journals or "law reviews." Only later was it adopted for general use by "practitioners," those people functioning in the "real world" of law practice. At the time *The Bluebook* was created, law review articles were generally typeset by professional printers who were able to use a format consisting of large and small capitals in which the first letter of a major word was displayed in a larger size capital letter than other letters in the word (for example, Trusts and Estates).

Practitioners' Approach

Because practitioners used typewriters to prepare briefs and documents rather than having them typeset by printers, they could not reproduce the large and small capital presentation dictated by *The Bluebook*, and as a result, practitioners began converting the large and small capital formats shown in *The Bluebook* to a simpler style, generally referred to as "ordinary roman type" (for example, Trusts and Estates). Ordinary roman type is the style most often used in books, newspapers, and magazines. Popular roman font styles include Times New Roman and Courier.

■ A Dual System of Citation

A twofold citation system thus developed with law reviews showing citations for state statutes, constitutions, book titles and authors, and periodical names in large and small capitals and practitioners showing those same citations in the simpler form, because practitioners were incapable at that time of producing large and small capitals on standard office typewriters.

Unfortunately, the dual system is generally not explained well (or even at all) to law or paralegal students or to those word processors who prepare briefs and other documents for practitioners. Many law students exit law school believing citations should be displayed in large and small capital letters, only to discover that they must learn to convert most of the examples found in *The Bluebook* to comport with the style used by practitioners.

You might wonder why the dual system persists when, with today's word processors, it is easily possible for practitioners to use the large and small capital format. That would result in a truly "uniform" system of citation with both law students and real-world practitioners presenting all citations in the same style. There is no good answer to this question. The dual system has persisted long after any need for it compels its use.

There are some other differences in the manner in which citations are presented in law review footnotes and in practitioners' documents. For example, return to the inside front and back covers of *The Bluebook* and note that in law review footnotes, full case names and book titles are not italicized or underscored, whereas they are italicized or underscored by practitioners. Other differences will be discussed later. For now, it is enough for you to know that court documents and legal memoranda never use large and small capitals.

The Bluebook's Advice (Rule 2; B1)

The Bluebook itself makes only passing references to the confusing and seldom understood rule requiring differing presentation styles when one is preparing academic writings, such as a law review article and when one is preparing nonacademic writings, such as a court document.

As discussed previously, the inside front and back covers of *The Bluebook* note that there is a difference in the typeface used in law review footnotes and that used by practitioners. Similarly, Rule 2 of *The Bluebook*, entitled Typefaces for Law Reviews, mentions the distinction; however, it merely instructs practitioners to assume the affirmative duty of substituting the typeface conventions found in the first section of *The Bluebook*, the Bluepages (a mere 24 pages), for those found in the remainder of *The Bluebook* (approximately 450 pages). Rule B1 states simply that "[l]arge and small caps are never used [by practitioners]." Thus, practitioners are primarily left to their own devices to figure out that most of *The Bluebook* is not for them. They will have to convert every instance of Large and Small Capitals to a simpler style, namely ordinary roman type.

Lesson: If you are a practitioner, never use Large and Small Capitals. In every instance in which you see such a presentation style in The Bluebook, *immediately convert it to the simpler style used by practitioners.*

If you have trouble remembering this rule, as you see examples throughout *The Bluebook*, ask yourself: Could I reproduce this presentation on an old-fashioned typewriter? If the answer is "no," it is a signal that the presentation was meant for printers who could manually typeset law review articles, not for practitioners.

Exercise for   Chapter 2

The following are examples found in The Bluebook. *Correct them for use by practitioners.*

1.   17 Am. Jur. 2d *Contracts* § 74 (1964).

_____

2.   N.M. Stat. Ann. § 4-44-7(G) (1983).

_____

3.   Fed. R. App. P. 2.

_____

4.   Restatement (Third) of Unfair Competition § 3 (1995).

_____

5.   4 Charles Alan Wright & Arthur R. Miller, Federal Practice and Procedure § 106 (2d ed. 1987).

_____

6. Kim Lane Scheppele, *Foreword: Telling Stories*, 87 MICH. L. REV. 2073, 2082 (1989).

_____

7. S. REP. NO. 84-2, at 7 (1955).

_____

3 Citation Form for Cases

■ Introduction

There are several important rules to know about cases, primarily rules dealing with case names, rules relating to citation form for state and federal court cases, and related rules about abbreviations and spacing in case (and other) citations.

The required elements of a full case citation are as follows:

- The name of the case
- A reference to the published source where the case can be located
- Parenthetical information consisting of the year of decision and an identification of the court that issued the decision (if such is not apparent from the name of the set itself)
- Parenthetical information, such as referring to a dissenting opinion (if any)
- Subsequent history of the case (if any)

■ **Case Names** (Rule 10.2; B4.1.1)

The rules relating to case names are discussed in *Bluebook* Rule 10.2 and
Bluepages B4.1.1. Some of the more critical rules are as follows:

- Case names can be <u>underscored</u> or *italicized,* although italics are more
  commonly used. Some writers have a strong preference for one
  approach rather than another. It is possible that older practitioners
  who began careers before the advent of computers prefer underscoring
  because the typewriters on which they prepared their documents were
  not capable of any other style, whereas younger practitioners might
  prefer italicizing because they are familiar with word processors that
  are capable of italicizing. Either approach is acceptable. Be consistent.
- When underscoring, underscore the entire case name using a solid
  unbroken line, including the "<u>v.</u>" (B4.1.1) and any procedural phrase
  such as "<u>In re.</u>"
- The "v." in a case citation is always a lowercase letter followed by a period.
- If the case names ends with an abbreviated word such as "<u>Inc.</u>" or
  "<u>Corp.,</u>" underscore or italicize the period in the abbreviation.
- Follow case names with a comma, which is neither underscored nor
  italicized.
- Give last names only of the parties in the case. Omit first names or
  initials, although always reproduce a business name scrupulously even
  if its name includes a person's name, as in *Carr v. Calvin Klein, Inc.*
- If there are multiple plaintiffs and defendants, list only the first
  plaintiff and the first defendant. Drop all other parties from the
  citation, and do not indicate that there are multiple parties by
  using an expression such as "et al.," a phrase meaning "and others."
- Do not identify the status of a party by including a term such as
  "plaintiff," "trustee," or "executor."
- Generally omit prepositional phrases of location (thus, the citation
  Brown v. Board of Education is correct, whereas *Brown v. Board of
  Education of Topeka, Kansas* is not).
- Criminal cases from your state will be titled *State v. Lee, People v. Lee,*
  or *Commonwealth v. Lee* (if the case originates in the Commonwealth
  of Kentucky, Massachusetts, Pennsylvania, or Virginia). When the
  criminal case leaves your jurisdiction and goes to the U.S. Supreme
  Court on appeal, its name will change to *Arizona v. Lee* or
  Pennsylvania v. Lee, probably to facilitate indexing of case names.
- If the case name includes two business designations, such as both
  "Inc." and "Co.," retain the first and strike the second.

- Do not abbreviate "United States" (or any state name) in a case name if it is the entire name of a party.
- Generally, omit "The" as the first word in a party's name. Thus, cite as *May Co. v. Daly* rather than *The May Co. v. Daly*.

Practice Tip

✓ Learn about cases from their names. The indication "v." in a case name indicates an adversarial matter. The indication "In re" in a case name usually indicates a nonadversarial matter, such as a bankruptcy, probate, or disbarment. It might also refer to large multidistrict litigation cases involving numerous parties, such as *In re Vitamin Antitrust Litigation* or *In re Teflon Products Liability Litigation*.

- If one of the parties is commonly referred to in spoken language by its initials rather than its full name (FBI, CIA, SEC), you may use that abbreviation in a case name and not include any periods (thus, *NLRB* is preferred and *N.L.R.B.* is not) (Rule 6.1(b)).

▮ **Abbreviations in Case Names**
(Rule 10.2.1(c); B4.1.1; Table T.6)

You might have already noticed that many case names are lengthy. What words can you abbreviate in a citation to save space? The answer depends on how the citation is presented to the reader.

Note that Rule 10.2.1(c) states that when case names appear in textual sentences, you may abbreviate only widely known acronyms (such as FBI and FCC) and the following eight well-known abbreviations: &, Ass'n, Bros., Co., Corp., Inc., Ltd., and No.

Now examine Table T.6 of *The Bluebook*, which tells you that "in citations" you abbreviate any of the more than 170 words listed, including words such as "Liab.," "Distrib.," and "Hous." Such words are to be abbreviated even if they are the first or only word in a case name. How can these two statements possibly be reconciled?

Consider the way in which legal writers make arguments. Most commonly, they will make a statement about the law in a declaratory sentence ending with a period and then follow that statement with a citation.

To avoid a rigid and rote approach, however, writers will often interweave citations into the middle of sentences. Which words can be abbreviated depends on which of these two styles is selected. The two governing rules are as follows:

- If your citation appears as part of a textual sentence (meaning that the citation is needed to make sense of the sentence), you should not distract your reader with odd-looking abbreviations. Thus, you may only abbreviate widely known acronyms (such as FBI and CIA) and the highly familiar eight words identified previously (such as "Inc." and "Co.").
- If, on the other hand, your citation stands alone as its own statement in support of (or in contradiction to) a previous declaration, unusual abbreviations will not distract the reader, and you must thus use any of the more than 170 words listed in Table T.6 (such as "Pub." and "Tech.").

Examples

- Punitive damages are recoverable in fraud actions. *W. Util. & Transp. Co. v. Lakewood Ref. Inc.*, 450 U.S. 24, 27 (1990).
- Although punitive damages are recoverable for fraud according to *Western Utility & Transportation Co. v. Lakewood Refining Inc.*, 450 U.S. 24, 27 (1990), those damages must bear a rational relationship to actual damages, *Peterson Indem. Co. v. Int'l Maint. Co.*, 451 U.S. 191, 199 (1992).

How will you remember this difficult rule? Consider that you already know this rule because you see it in practice everyday. You seldom, if ever, see abbreviations in novels or magazine articles, even commonly used abbreviations such as "St." for "Street." Abbreviations typically end with periods and are thus jarring and distracting to readers if they appear in the middle of a sentence. Thus, remember that if your citation is part of a sentence, don't distract your reader with odd-looking abbreviations; however, if your citation "stands alone," the reader doesn't need it to make sense of the sentence and will not be bothered by abbreviated words.

Practice Tips

✓ Write across the top of Table T.6 of your *Bluebook* the note "For Stand-Alone Citations Only" to remind you that the listed abbreviations can only be used when your citation stands alone as its own sentence.

✓ Photocopy Table T.6 and keep it nearby. This is the table that cite-checkers use most often, so don't spend time searching for it in *The Bluebook*. Keep it available on your desktop or tape it to the edge of your computer.

✓ In case names, abbreviate states, cities, and other geographical units as shown in Table T.10 (unless they are the entire name of a party). Thus, *Parr v. Univ. of Va.* is correct for a "stand-alone" citation but *Parr v. Va.* is not.

✓ Unless otherwise indicated in Table T.6, to pluralize an abbreviation just add an "s" to the abbreviation (before the period), such as changing "Hosp." to "Hosps."

✓ If one of the eight well-known words (such as Co. or Inc.) begins a party's name, it cannot be abbreviated.

Until 2000, *The Bluebook* prohibited abbreviating the first word in a plaintiff's or defendant's name. The current rule requires you to abbreviate any of the words in Table T.6, even if that word is the first word in a party's name (in a "stand-alone" citation) as shown in the first example above. Many law firms and practitioners dislike this rule and continue to follow the prior rule by never abbreviating the first word in a party's name.

State Court Cases (Rule 10.3; B4.1.3)

Background

To master citation form for state court cases, one must understand how cases are published. Cases are published either officially (meaning their publication is mandated by a statute) or unofficially (meaning they are published without such authority). Years ago, nearly all states mandated that their appellate court cases that advanced legal theory be published. The sets of books that collected these decisions were called *reports* and generally were indicated by a state abbreviation ("Ga." for cases from Georgia, "Cal." for cases from California, and so forth). Because publication of these sets was government approved, they were called "official."

Because what courts decide is a matter of public record and is not subject to copyright protection, anyone can copy cases that are already published, print the cases, and bind them, perhaps adding some editorial features. Such a set is *unofficial*, meaning its publication is not authorized by the state legislature but is rather the result of some independent act of a third party.

Such action was undertaken by two brothers named John and Horatio West in the late 1800s. They republished cases that had already been published officially, grouped them together in various geographical units, and began selling the sets to practitioners. The company, now West, a Thomson Reuters business (hereinafter "West") thus produces the *North Western Reporter*, which publishes cases from North Dakota, South Dakota, Nebraska, Minnesota, Iowa, Wisconsin, and Michigan. A Michigan case that appears in the *North Western Reporter* is the same as the Michigan case published in the official *Michigan Reports*, although certain editorial enhancements may vary from set to set. Thus, the case *Brown v. Whitney* might be located at 432 Mich. 13 and at 209 N.W.2d 421. The two citations are called *parallel* citations.

West also produces other sets of books that arrange cases published in certain geographical units. (See Figure 3-1.)

After West created the seven geographical or regional units, it decided that certain states produced so much case law they should have their own sets of books, and so it created the *California Reporter*, the *New York Supplement*, and *Illinois Decisions* (for cases from those states). Thus, for example, a newer California Supreme Court case may have three parallel citations: a reference to its publication in the official *California Reports*, a reference to its publication in the *Pacific Reporter*, and a reference to its publication in the more newly created specialized set, *California Reporter*.

Some practitioners might prefer to buy the official *California Reports* and others might prefer to obtain access to cases from surrounding states by purchasing the *Pacific Reporter*.

Practice Tip

✓ A color-coded map showing the grouping of states in West's National Reporter System can be found on West's website at http://lawschool.westlaw.com/federalcourt/nationalreporter page.asp.

Citation Form

For nearly 70 years, *The Bluebook* required that practitioners provide all parallel citations when citing state court cases, reasoning that the author could not possibly know what set of books the reader had in his or her law office or judge's chambers, and thus, authors should provide all citations to enable a reader to locate easily any cited case. Writers were required to give the official citation first, followed by a comma and then the unofficial citation.

Atlantic Reporter (A., A.2d)	Connecticut, Delaware, Maine, Maryland, New Hampshire, New Jersey, Pennsylvania, Rhode Island, Vermont, Washington, D.C.
North Eastern Reporter (N.E., N.E.2d)	Illinois, Indiana, Massachusetts, New York, Ohio
South Eastern Reporter (S.E., S.E.2d)	Georgia, North Carolina, South Carolina, Virginia, West Virginia
Southern Reporter (So., So. 2d, So. 3d)	Alabama, Florida, Louisiana, Mississippi
North Western Reporter (N.W., N.W.2d)	Iowa, Michigan, Minnesota, Nebraska, North Dakota, South Dakota, Wisconsin
South Western Reporter (S.W., S.W.2d, S.W.3d)	Arkansas, Kentucky, Missouri, Tennessee, Texas
Pacific Reporter (P., P.2d, P.3d)	Alaska, Arizona, California, Colorado, Hawaii, Idaho, Kansas, Montana, Nevada, New Mexico, Oklahoma, Oregon, Utah, Washington, Wyoming

Figure 3-1 West's National Reporter System for State Court Cases

Although the rule relating to citation of state court cases has been revised a bit since 1991, the current rule (from the Nineteenth Edition of *The Bluebook*) is as follows:

- If court rules require parallel citations, you must give them (typically giving the official citation first, followed by the unofficial citation(s)).
- Unless court rules require parallel citations, cite solely to the regional reporter (for example, P.2d or N.W.2d), and give a reference to the state, the deciding court, and the year of decision parenthetically. (See B4.1.3 and Rules 10.3.1 and 10.4.)

Thus, if you are citing a Virginia case in a document sent to a court that requires parallel citations, you must give them (listing the official citation first and the unofficial second). If you are citing the same case in any other instance, give only the regional citation. As always, if local rules exist regarding citation form, they supersede *The Bluebook* rules.

How will you know which is the official citation that must be placed first and which is the unofficial citation that must be placed second? The official citation includes an abbreviation for the state (such as "Cal." or "Ga."), whereas the unofficial citation is generally a regional abbreviation (such as "A." for "Atlantic," "S.E." for South Eastern, and so forth). The courts of each state are listed in *The Bluebook* in Table T.1 from highest court to lowest court.

Although the state-by-state summary in Table T.1 provides instruction on citing state court cases, the information in Table T.1 is directed to citation form for law review footnotes. Practitioners should thus follow the format and examples given in the Bluepages section of *The Bluebook*.

Remember that cases from California, Illinois, and New York can have three parallel citations, and you must order the citation as outlined in Table T.1 in *The Bluebook*.

Examples

- *Samson Corp. v. Bailey*, 302 Va. 118, 671 S.E.2d 909 (1990). This form is used when a court rule requires parallel citations.
- *Samson Corp. v. Bailey*, 671 S.E.2d 909 (Va. 1990). This form is used in any instance other than when a court rule requires parallel citations.

Parentheticals for State Court Cases
(Rule 10.4(b); B4.1.3)

Note the parenthetical given in the preceding second example. Without the indication of "Va." in the parenthetical, the reader would have no idea which of the five states in the *South Eastern Reporter* issued the decision. The reader must be given this critical piece of information.

If the parenthetical merely gives the abbreviation for the state (such as "Cal." or "Va."), it is an indication that the case is from the highest court in that state. (Rule 10.4(b)). If the case was decided by a court other than the highest court, you must indicate such in the parenthetical, generally by providing the abbreviation "Ct. App." For example, the citation *State v. Bowie*, 429 P.2d 136 (Cal. Ct. App. 1958), indicates the case is from the intermediate appellate court in California, whereas the citation *Franks v. Park*, 436

P.2d 102 (Cal. 1992), indicates the case was decided by the highest court in California, the California Supreme Court. Similarly, "(Kan. 1996)" indicates a 1996 decision of the Kansas Supreme Court, whereas "(Kan. Ct. App. 1996)" indicates a 1996 decision of the Kansas Court of Appeals.

When the deciding state is clear from the name of the official reporter set (as it is in "Cal." or "Kan."), it is not needed in a parenthetical (see the preceding first example). Similarly, you do not need to indicate the name of a court if the deciding court is the highest one in that state. Do not indicate the department or district that decided a case unless that information is particularly relevant. Note that there is a space before the parenthetical is opened.

Remember that local rules always supersede *Bluebook* rules. For example, although *The Bluebook* clearly states that there is no need to indicate which department or court district decided a case unless it is of particular relevance (Rule 10.4(b)), local Florida rules require such. Similarly, although *The Bluebook* shows the abbreviation for the set *Washington Reports* as "Wash.," local court rules require that the set be shown as "Wn." Most local rules can be accessed through MegaLaw at http://www.megalaw.com.

In a few states, including Arizona, Hawaii, Idaho, New Mexico, South Carolina, and Wisconsin, cases from the state supreme court and from the state court of appeals are published in one set. For example, *Idaho Reports* now publishes decisions from the Idaho Supreme Court and the Idaho Court of Appeals. Because the name of the set, *Idaho Reports*, does not tell which court decided the case, additional information is required in the parenthetical, when referring to appellate court cases, as follows: *Bell v. Hall*, 204 Idaho 14, 611 P.2d 84 (Ct. App. 1990). Note that no reference to "Idaho" is given in the parenthetical because the reader can easily tell which state decided the case.

Some states, including Alabama, Oklahoma, Tennessee, and Texas, have or have had separate courts of criminal appeals (and often separate courts of civil appeals). Citations to those cases would be given as follows:

State v. Harris, 82 Tenn. Crim. App. 141, 203 S.W.2d 18 (1968)
(if a court rule requires parallel citations).

or

State v. Harris, 203 S.W.2d 18 (Tenn. Crim. App. 1968).

Finally, some jurisdictions (the District of Columbia, Maine, Montana, Nevada, New Hampshire, Rhode Island, South Dakota, Vermont, West Virginia, and Wyoming) have no intermediate appellate courts. In those states, all citations are to the jurisdiction's highest court (usually called its supreme court).

How will you know which states have no intermediate appellate court? Review Table T.1 of *The Bluebook* (for example, see page 251 of *The Bluebook*, which lists only a supreme court for New Hampshire), or access the website for the National Center for State Courts (http://www.ncsconline.org), which provides court structure charts for each state.

Practice Tip

✓ Nearly all states call their highest court "the supreme court" (or something highly similar). Three jurisdictions, however, have different names for their highest courts: the District of Columbia, Maryland, and New York all title their highest courts "the court of appeals."

Discontinuation of Some Official Reports

Because West's unofficial reporters became so successful, and many practitioners preferred the West reporters to their own official state reports, a number of states (generally the less populous ones) ceased publishing officially. For cases from these states, you will only be able to cite to West's unofficial regional reporter (and then provide the appropriate parenthetical information). You will not be able to include an official citation because one does not exist after the date official publication ceased. For cases decided prior to the date official publication ceased, follow the normal citation rules for state court cases discussed previously (namely, give parallel citations only when local rules require).

How can one determine if a state has discontinued official publication? Table T.1 of *The Bluebook* provides the answer. For example, note that the entry for West Virginia on page 272 states that the *West Virginia Reports* covers cases from "1864–date" and page 264 indicates that the *Rhode Island Reports* covers cases from "1828–1980." Such is an indication that West Virginia is still publishing officially but Rhode Island ceased official publication in 1980. Thus, for cases decided in Rhode Island after 1980, the citation form is always as follows:

Wong v. Harris, 590 A.2d 118 (R.I. 1985). (Note: For cases from Rhode Island prior to 1980, you might need to include both parallel citations, namely to R.I. and to A. or A.2d, if local rules require parallel citations.)

See the Appendix, Examples of State Cases and Statutes, for sample citations for all states and the District of Columbia. See Figure 3-2 for a table of discontinued official state court reports.

State	Year of Discontinuation	State	Year of Discontinuation
Alabama	1976	Minnesota	1977
Alaska	Never published cases officially	Mississippi	1966
Arkansas	2009	Missouri	1956
Colorado	1980	North Dakota	1953
Delaware	1966	Oklahoma	1953
District of Columbia	1941	Rhode Island	1980
Florida	1948	South Dakota	1976
Indiana	1981	Tennessee	1972
Iowa	1968	Texas	1962
Kentucky	1951	Utah	1974
Louisiana	1971	Wyoming	1959
Maine	1965		

Figure 3-2 Table of Discontinued Official State Court Reports

■ Public Domain Citations
(Rule 10.3.3)

Ever-increasing numbers of cases and statutes have begun appearing on the Internet (often on courts' websites). However, the traditional method of citing to volume and page numbers in printed books of case reports cannot be used effectively for new opinions appearing on the Internet because the printed case books are not published for several weeks (or even months) after an opinion is released on the Internet or on a court's website. Therefore, both the American Bar Association (ABA) and the American Association of Law Libraries (AALL) have recommended that courts adopt a uniform citation system that is equally adaptable whether authorities are located in conventional printed materials or through electronic means. The proposed system is variously called "public domain," "vendor neutral," or "medium neutral" because the citation will look the same whether the source is found in print or electronic media. Several states require that citations to their state court cases be in public domain format.

The *Bluebook* Approach (Rule 10.3.3)

Bluebook Rule 10.3.3 states that if it is available, a parallel citation to the appropriate regional reporter *must* be provided in addition to a public domain citation. Thus, the public domain citation really only replaces the official citation. The citation should include the case name, year of decision, the state's two-character postal code (given in Table T.1.3), the court abbreviation (given in Table T.7) unless the court is the state's highest court, sequential number of the decision, an uppercase "U" if the decision is unpublished, and a paragraph number when referring to specific material in the case.

Example

- *Wade v. Lee*, 2003 ND 138, ¶ 7, 670 N.W.2d 18, 22.

Which states have adopted official public domain citation formats such that you would use the format described herein rather than the usual approach consisting of case name, official citation, regional citation, and year of decision? At the time of publication of the Sixteenth Edition of *The Bluebook* in 1996, only Louisiana had adopted a public domain citation format. Since that time, Arkansas, Maine, Mississippi, Montana, New Mexico, North Dakota, Ohio, Oklahoma, Pennsylvania (for Superior Court cases only), South Dakota, Utah, Vermont, Wisconsin, and Wyoming have adopted public domain citation systems, but other states might be considering adoption. If you cite cases from these states, check state and local court rules regarding citation form. In the absence of any information, follow the format shown in *The Bluebook*. Table T.1.3 provides an example for each of the above-listed states. Additional information can be located at the website for the ABA Legal Technology Resource Center at http://www.abanet.org/tech/ltrc/research/citation/home.html and at the website for the American Association of Law Libraries at http://www.aallnet.org/committee/citation/ucg/index.html.

There is much variation from state to state in spacing and abbreviations in these public domain citations. Some states neither underscore nor italicize case names in public domain citations. Some states show a space between a paragraph symbol and its number and others do not. Additional information might be available at your state's home page. Access the website for MegaLaw (http://www.megalaw.com) and then select "State Law" and review your state's court rules. Information about citation form and other state-specific rules might be provided at the site. Additionally, Table T.1.3 provides references to each state's judicial website, and local rules relating to citation form are found in *Bluebook* Table BT2.

Note that *The Bluebook* discussion of public domain citations only relates to state court cases. In fact, interest in public domain citations appears to be waning; since 2003, only Arkansas has adopted a public domain citation format. As to federal cases, there is no indication in *The Bluebook* that using a public domain citation for any federal case is appropriate. In fact, most federal court judges are adamantly opposed to public domain citations, primarily because the burden of numbering paragraphs and assigning sequential opinion numbers would fall on the courts themselves.

▤ Federal Court Cases
(B4.1.3; Table T.1)

Background

To understand how to cite cases from our federal courts, you must first have a basic understanding of our federal court structure. The trial courts in our federal system are our United States District Courts. These district courts may handle a wide variety of cases, from bank robbery to free speech to copyright cases. There are more than 90 district courts for the United States and its territories. Each state has at least one district court, and if a state has a heavy caseload or comprises a significant geographic area, it might have more than one district court. Thus, New Jersey has one district court and California has four district courts. (See Figure 3-3, which identifies district courts and U.S. courts of appeals.)

Litigants who lose a case in the district court can appeal an adverse decision to our intermediate federal courts of appeals. The United States is divided into 13 areas, often called "circuits," with various states being grouped into a circuit. Thus, New York, Connecticut, and Vermont are in the Second Circuit, and most western states are in the Ninth Circuit. We have 11 numbered circuits, one for the District of Columbia, and one called the Federal Circuit that primarily handles patent matters and appeals from administrative agencies. (See Figure 3-4 for a map of the 13 federal judicial circuits.)

State	District Court	Circuit
Alabama	M.D. Ala.	11th Cir.
	N.D. Ala.	
	S.D. Ala.	
Alaska	D. Alaska	9th Cir.
Arizona	D. Ariz.	9th Cir.
Arkansas	E.D. Ark.	8th Cir.
	W.D. Ark.	
California	C.D. Cal.	9th Cir.
	E.D. Cal.	
	N.D. Cal.	
	S.D. Cal.	
Colorado	D. Colo.	10th Cir.
Connecticut	D. Conn.	2d Cir.
Delaware	D. Del.	3d Cir.
District of Columbia	D.D.C.	D.C. Cir
Florida	M.D. Fla.	11th Cir.
	N.D. Fla.	
	S.D. Fla.	
Georgia	M.D. Ga.	11th Cir.
	N.D. Ga.	
	S.D. Ga.	
Hawaii	D. Haw.	9th Cir.
Idaho	D. Idaho	9th Cir.
Illinois	C.D. Ill.	7th Cir.
	N.D. Ill.	
	S.D. Ill.	
Indiana	N.D. Ind.	7th Cir.
	S.D. Ind.	
Iowa	N.D. Iowa	8th Cir.
	S.D. Iowa	
Kansas	D. Kan.	10th Cir.
Kentucky	E.D. Ky.	6th Cir.
	W.D. Ky.	
Louisiana	E.D. La.	5th Cir.
	M.D. La.	
	W.D. La.	
Maine	D. Me.	1st Cir.
Maryland	D. Md.	4th Cir.
Massachusetts	D. Mass.	1st Cir.
Michigan	E.D. Mich.	6th Cir.
	W.D. Mich.	
Minnesota	D. Minn.	8th Cir.
Mississippi	N.D. Miss.	5th Cir.
	S.D. Miss.	
Missouri	E.D. Mo.	8th Cir.
	W.D. Mo.	

Figure 3-3 District Courts and U.S. Courts of Appeal

State	District	Circuit	State	District	Circuit
Montana	D. Mont.	9th Cir.	South Carolina	D.S.C.	4th Cir.
Nebraska	D. Neb.	8th Cir.	South Dakota	D.S.D.	8th Cir.
Nevada	D. Nev.	9th Cir.	Tennessee	E.D. Tenn.	6th Cir.
New Hampshire	D.N.H.	1st Cir.		M.D. Tenn.	
New Jersey	D.N.J.	3d Cir.		W.D. Tenn.	
New Mexico	D.N.M.	10th Cir.	Texas	E.D. Tex.	5th Cir.
New York	E.D.N.Y.	2d Cir.		N.D. Tex.	
	N.D.N.Y.			S.D. Tex.	
	S.D.N.Y.			W.D. Tex.	
	W.D.N.Y.		Utah	D. Utah	10th Cir.
North Carolina	E.D.N.C.	4th Cir.	Vermont	D. Vt.	2d Cir.
	M.D.N.C.		Virginia	E.D. Va.	4th Cir.
	W.D.N.C.			W.D. Va.	
North Dakota	D.N.D.	8th Cir.	Washington	E.D. Wash.	9th Cir.
Ohio	N.D. Ohio	6th Cir.		W.D. Wash.	
	S.D. Ohio		West Virginia	N.D. W. Va.	4th Cir.
Oklahoma	E.D. Okla.	10th Cir.		S.D. W. Va.	
	N.D. Okla.		Wisconsin	E.D. Wis.	7th Cir.
	W.D. Okla.			W.D. Wis.	
Oregon	D. Or.	9th Cir.	Wyoming	D. Wyo.	10th Cir.
Pennsylvania	E.D. Pa.	3d Cir.	U.S. Court of Appeals for the Federal Circuit		Fed. Cir.
	M.D. Pa.				
	W.D. Pa.		U.S. Court of Appeals for the District of Columbia		D.C. Cir.
Rhode Island	D.R.I.	1st Cir.			

Figure 3-3 District Courts and U.S. Courts of Appeal (*continued*)

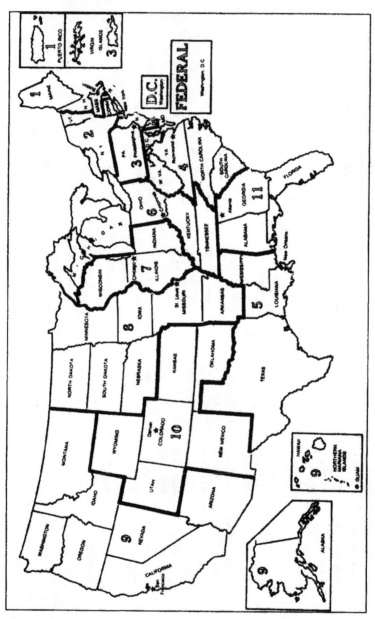

Figure 3-4 The Thirteen Federal Judicial Circuits. *See* 28 U.S.C.A. § 41 (West 2004)

A litigant who loses in a federal circuit may then attempt to appeal the adverse decision to the U.S. Supreme Court. However, the Supreme Court generally has the discretion to determine which cases it accepts for review and which it does not. When it accepts a case for review it "grants certiorari" (certiorari is a Latin word meaning "to be fully informed"). If it refuses to take the case, as it does more than 95 percent of the time, it "denies certiorari."

Although there are federal courts other than those discussed here (tax courts, military justice courts, and bankruptcy courts, for example), this text addresses citation form for the most commonly encountered federal cases. Use Table T.1 of *The Bluebook* to determine citation form for cases from federal courts other than those discussed herein.

Citation of Federal Court Cases (B4.1.3; Table T.1)

District Court Cases

Ordinarily, trial court cases in this country are not published. There are simply too many of them. West, however, decided to create a set of books to publish some cases from the district courts (the trial courts in our federal system) because important federal or constitutional issues can be raised in such cases. The set West created is called the *Federal Supplement* (abbreviated as "F. Supp." or F. Supp. 2d"). It is unofficial, and there are no parallel citations for cases from the federal district courts. Every citation, however, must include a reference to the specific deciding court, so include the district court information in the parenthetical with the date.

Examples

Corey v. Shea, 889 F. Supp. 16 (E.D. Va. 1987).
Joshua Tree Ltd. v. Baker, 10 F. Supp. 2d 190 (S.D.N.Y. 1999).

Courts of Appeals Cases

At present, there is only one set of books that reports published cases from the intermediate courts of appeals: *Federal Reporter* (abbreviated as "F.," "F.2d," or "F.3d"), an unofficial set published by West. Thus, you need not worry about parallel citations for cases from the intermediate courts of appeals. Every citation, however, must include a reference to the specific deciding court, so always include the circuit information in the parenthetical with the date.

Figure 3-5 provides a diagram of the federal court system.

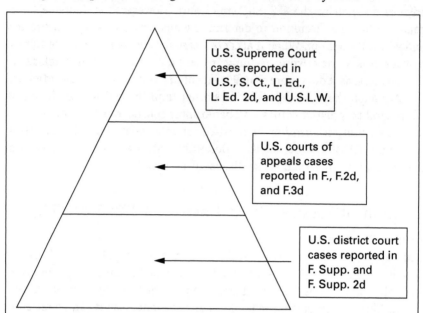

U.S. Supreme Court cases reported in U.S., S. Ct., L. Ed., L. Ed. 2d, and U.S.L.W.

U.S. courts of appeals cases reported in F., F.2d, and F.3d

U.S. district court cases reported in F. Supp. and F. Supp. 2d

Figure 3-5   Federal Court System (excluding administrative and specialized courts)

Examples

Ray v. Libby Co., 789 F.2d 118 (2d Cir. 1994).
Atl. Mgmt. Co. v. Moe, 15 F.3d 931 (Fed. Cir. 1998).

A newly created set published by West, *Federal Appendix*, reports decisions since 2001 from most of the intermediate courts of appeal that have not been designated for publication. Federal courts now allow citation to unpublished cases, but always check your local rules relating to citing such cases. A case reported in *Federal Appendix* would be cited as follows: *United States v. Drayer*, 364 F. App'x 716 (2d Cir. 2010).

U.S. Supreme Court Cases

Cases from the U.S. Supreme Court are published in a variety of sources. They are published officially in a set called *United States Reports*, and they are published unofficially in three places: by West in a set called *Supreme*

Court Reporter, by LexisNexis in a set called *Lawyers Edition* (or *Lawyers Edition, Second Series*), and in a weekly journal called *United States Law Week*. Additionally, U.S. Supreme Court cases can be located through Lexis, Westlaw, and on the Internet at the Court's website at http://www.supremecourt.gov.

Although there are thus at least four parallel citations for U.S. Supreme Court cases, *The Bluebook* rule is direct: Cite to *United States Reports* (U.S.) if the case is published in that set. If not, cite to *Supreme Court Reporter* (S. Ct.), *Lawyers Edition* (L. Ed. or L. Ed. 2d), or *United States Law Week* (U.S.L.W.) in that order of preference. Do not give a parallel citation.

If you are wondering why a case would not be published in the official *United States Reports*, remember that the set is official. It is published under government authority. The commercial publishers release volumes much more quickly. Thus, for newer cases, the official citation might not yet be available, requiring you to cite to one of the other sets.

Examples

Farley v. Galloway, 501 U.S. 699 (1998).
Hall v. Porter, 239 S. Ct. 993 (2010).

The second citation would be for a case not yet published in the official *United States Reports*.

Practice Tip

✓ Some practitioners use the form *Taylor v. Green*, _____ U.S. _____, 241 S. Ct. 901 (2010) for recent cases, presumably to indicate to a reader that although an official citation will eventually exist, it is not available yet, and thus the author is providing the reader with the "default" citation from the *Supreme Court Reporter*. Although this technique is commonly encountered in practice, there is no authority for it in *The Bluebook*. Check your firm or office practice.

Public Domain Citations

Although the ABA has recommended a public domain citation system for federal cases, such a system has not been adopted or mandated by any federal courts. In fact, most federal courts adamantly oppose such citations.

Practice Tip

✓ Color-coded maps of West's National Reporter System and the U.S. Courts of Appeal are available on the Internet. Bookmark the following websites so these maps are readily available to you.

National Reporter System Map:
http://lawschool.westlaw.com/federalcourt/
    nationalreporterpage.asp
U.S. Courts of Appeal Map:
http://www.uscourts.gov

■ Subsequent and Prior History
(Rule 10.7; B4.1.6; Table T.8)

Subsequent History

When you "Shepardize" or "KeyCite" a case to determine whether it is still good law, you will find the subsequent history and treatment of the case as later courts or cases have discussed it. According to *Bluebook* Rule 10.7, you are ethically obligated to give the entire subsequent history of a case. Nevertheless, omit the following subsequent history:

- Denials of certiorari or denials of similar discretionary appeals, unless your lower court case is less than two years old or the denial is particularly relevant.
- History on remand (when a case is returned or remanded to a trial court by an appellate court to ensure the lower court complies with the appellate court's instructions), unless relevant.
- Denials of discretionary appeals, such as rehearings (when a disappointed party requests that a court reconsider or rehear a case),

unless relevant. Because rehearings are so often requested and seldom granted, generally omit this information.

Until the Sixteenth Edition of *The Bluebook* in 1996, one was always required to include a denial of certiorari. The Sixteenth, Seventeenth, Eighteenth, and Nineteenth Editions of *The Bluebook* instruct writers to omit such denials unless the case is recent (less than two years old) or the denial is particularly relevant. Some practitioners object to the new rule, believing that the denial of certiorari sends a signal to a reader that a case is final and is, thus, always relevant. Determine if your firm or office has a policy regarding this matter.

How does one indicate subsequent history? When you Shepardize the case and find the subsequent history, consult Table T.8 of *The Bluebook* for the appropriate abbreviation and then cite as follows:

Examples

Young v. Barr Co., 45 F.3d 18 (D.C. Cir. 2009), *cert. denied*, 530 U.S. 166 (2010). (Note: If underscoring, use a solid unbroken line for cert. denied.)

Jacobs v. Nelson, 789 F. Supp. 16 (D.N.J. 1994), *rev'd*, 904 F.2d 18 (3d Cir. 1995).

Practice Tip

✓ If the date in the second parenthetical will be the same as that in the first, strike the date from the first parenthetical and retain it only in the second (Rule 10.5(d)) as follows:

Li v. Li, 44 F.3d 21 (9th Cir.), *aff'd*, 519 U.S. 901 (1998).

Prior History

Virtually all cases from the U.S. Supreme Court (and the highest courts in a state) have prior history because they were not originally decided by the Supreme Court, but came to the Court from lower appellate courts. Are you required to give the prior history of such a case or other cases with prior history? No. Only give prior history if it is significant to the point you are making.

Practice Tips

✓ **Federal cases:** You never need to give parallel citations for federal
    cases. When citing to U.S. Supreme Court cases, cite only to U.S.
    (if the case is published in that set). Lower federal court cases
    have no parallel citations.

✓ **State cases:** Give a parallel citation only if a local rule requires such.
    Otherwise, cite to the regional reporter and then show the state
    and court of decision in the parenthetical with the year of decision
    (although you may omit the name of the court if the case is from
    the highest court in that jurisdiction). Remember that more than
    20 states no longer publish their cases officially; for these states,
    it is no longer possible to include a parallel citation.

■ Series of Court Reports

You may have noticed that some citations are to "F." and others are to "F.2d"
or "F.3d." Similarly, some citations are to "N.E." and others are to "N.E.2d."
Why? As publishers publish cases in the court reports, the volume numbers
of the sets keep increasing. Probably to ensure that the volume number does
not become confusingly high, the publishers eventually stop publishing an
initial set (such as F. or N.E.) and begin publishing a new series (such as F.2d
or N.E.2d). Still other sets can have higher series numbers such as Cal. 4th.
You do not need to know when the series numbers switch over. You need
only know that any case in F.3d is newer than any case in F.2d, and likewise
any case in F.2d is newer than any case in F.

Note that the abbreviation for "second" in legal citations is always "2d"
(rather than the nonlegal abbreviation "2nd" that is commonly used). Similarly, the abbreviation for "third" in legal citations is always "3d" and not
"3rd." Other abbreviations, such as those for 4th, 5th, and so forth, are
identical to those used in nonlegal writing.

Practice Tip

✓ You might have noticed that when you type ordinals such as
    "6th" or "4th" when referring to the Sixth or Fourth Circuit
    Courts of Appeal, your word processor may elevate the "th"

to superscript form (as in "6ᵗʰ" or "4ᵗʰ"). *The Bluebook* flatly prohibits the use of superscripts (Rule 6.2(b)).

Incorrect: (8ᵗʰ Cir. 2004)
Correct: (8th Cir. 2004)

✓ For certain versions of Microsoft Word, you can disable this feature on your word processor by selecting "Tools," then "AutoCorrect," and then "AutoFormat As You Type." Clear the appropriate check box relating to superscripts.

▉ Spacing in Citations (Rule 6.1(a))

The following spacing rules apply to all citations, not merely cases. There are three spacing rules:

- If a single capital letter is followed by another single capital letter, close them up together with no spaces (for purposes of this rule, numerals and ordinals are treated as single capitals), and close up initials in personal names.

  A.2d   S.W.   U.S.   F.3d   N.W.2d   A.L.R.5th   J.C. Jones

- Multiple letter abbreviations (such as "Cal." and "Supp.") are preceded and followed by spaces.

  Cal. App.   F. Supp. 2d   So. 2d   S. Ct.   D. Minn.   Fed. R. Civ. P.

- Be careful with the abbreviations for periodicals. The spacing rule requires you to determine if one or more of the capitals refers to the name of an institutional entity, such as a school. If so, set the capital or capitals referring to the entity apart from other single capitals. Because this rule is so confusing, you should simply consult Table T.13, which gives abbreviations for more than 700 periodicals, and mimic the spacing you see. (Note, however, that you must convert the large and small capitals to ordinary roman type.)

  Correct: N.C. L. Rev.   N.M. L. Rev.

Exercise for ## Chapter 3

Correct the following citations. You might need to supply or create missing information, such as dates and page numbers. Either make up numbers and dates or use the form "xxx" as in "xxx P.2d xxx." There might be more than one thing wrong with the citation.

Case Names

1. Renee Burnette versus M.L. Parker

     _____

2. N.P. Hicks, Jr. vs. Andrew J. Koch and Alan R. Ladwig

     _____

3. State of Ohio versus Manufacturers Engineering Coalition Association, a state court case (Assume the citation appears as a "stand-alone" citation.)

     _____

4. State of Ohio versus Manufacturers Engineering Coalition Association, a state court case (Assume the citation appears as part of a textual sentence.)

     _____

5. Southern Casualty and Indemnity Company versus USA (Cite first assuming the citation appears in a textual sentence and then cite as a stand-alone citation.)

     _____

6. James & Susan Lovell versus the Federal Communications Commission

     _____

7. Judith D. Harris vs. O'Hara, et al.

     _____

State Court Cases

8. McBride v. Murphy, 304 Kansas Reports 123 (2006) (Assume the citation appears in a brief submitted to a court requiring parallel citations.)

---

9. Danielson v. Franklin Corporation, 86 New York Reports, Second Series, at page 111, 640 New York Supplement, Second Series 766, 690 North Eastern Reporter, Second Series, 211 (2004) (Cite first assuming the citation appears in a brief submitted to a court requiring parallel citations and then cite assuming the citation appears in a letter to a client.)

---

10. Smith v. Michaelson, a 2009 case from the Connecticut Appellate Court (Cite first assuming the citation appears in a brief submitted to a court requiring parallel citations and then cite assuming the citation appears in a letter to a client.)

---

11. Ruiz v. Jacobsen Brothers, a 2007 case from the Iowa Supreme Court.

---

12. Parker v. Tech Inc., a 2006 case from the Iowa Court of Appeals.

---

13. Simmons & Simmons Co. v. Gregson, a 2009 case from the Arizona Court of Appeals (Assume court rules require parallel citations.)

14. Give the public domain citation (with pinpoints) for the 2004 Oklahoma case *Mansfield versus Harrison*.

Federal Cases and Subsequent History

15. Knudson v. Micro Strategy Inc., 540 United States Reports 544, 213 Lawyers Edition, Second Series 967, 203 Supreme Court Reporter 118 (2005).

---

16. Mitchell v. ABC Co., a 2009 Third Circuit case located in volume 311 of the Federal Reporter, Third Series, at page 802 (Assume certiorari was denied for this case by the U.S. Supreme Court in 2010.)

---

17. Pritchett v. Bailey, 799 Federal Reporter, Second Series, page 100, decided by the Ninth Circuit Court of Appeals in 2008 and reversed by the U.S. Supreme Court in that same year.

---

18. Alvarez v. Nickles, a 2008 case from the U.S. District Court for the Central District of California.

---

19. Harvey v. Phillips, a 2001 case from the U.S. District Court for the District of Delaware and affirmed in 2002 by the Third Circuit Court of Appeals.

Spacing

20. 101 Federal Reporter, Third Series 901

---

21. 11 American Law Reports, Sixth Series 489

---

22. 14 Southern Reporter, Third Series 399

---

23. 689 Pacific Reporter, Second Series 320

---

24. 40 Federal Supplement, Second Series 430

---

25. 42 Boston University Law Review 607

---

26. 12 New York University Environmental Law Journal 977

---

27. 344 New York Supplement, Second Series 175

---

28. U.S. District Court for the Southern District of Ohio

---

29. U.S. District Court for the District of New Jersey

---

4 Citation Form for Statutes, Legislative Materials, Uniform Acts, Court Rules, and Constitutions

▒ **Statutes** (Rule 12; B5)

Federal Statutes

Federal statutes are published in three separate sources. They are published officially in a set called the *United States Code*, and they are published unofficially by West in a set called *United States Code Annotated* and by LexisNexis in a set called *United States Code Service*. The basic citation form is the same for each set.

A citation must include the following elements:

- Reference to the title within the set
- Reference to the abbreviated name of the set
- Citation to the relevant statutory section

- Parenthetical that includes a year and, if you cite to anything other than the official set, a reference to the publisher of the unofficial set (although practitioners nearly always omit the entire parenthetical)

Thus, a reference to "17 U.S.C. § 107 (2006)" directs a reader to title 17 of the *United States Code*, section 107. See Figure 4-1 for a listing of titles for federal statutes.

1. General Provisions
2. The Congress
3. The President
4. Flag and Seal, Seat of Government, and the States
5. Government Organization and Employees
6. Surety Bonds
7. Agriculture
8. Aliens and Nationality
9. Arbitration
10. Armed Forces
11. Bankruptcy
12. Banks and Banking
13. Census
14. Coast Guard
15. Commerce and Trade
16. Conservation
17. Copyrights
18. Crimes and Criminal Procedure
19. Customs Duties
20. Education
21. Food and Drugs
22. Foreign Relations and Intercourse
23. Highways
24. Hospitals and Asylums
25. Indians
26. Internal Revenue Code
27. Intoxicating Liquors
28. Judiciary and Judicial Procedure
29. Labor
30. Mineral Lands and Mining
31. Money and Finance
32. National Guard
33. Navigation and Navigable Waters
34. Navy (see Title 10, Armed Forces)
35. Patents
36. Patriotic Societies and Observances
37. Pay and Allowances of the Uniformed Services
38. Veterans' Benefits
39. Postal Service
40. Public Buildings, Property, and Works
41. Public Contracts
42. The Public Health and Welfare
43. Public Lands
44. Public Printing and Documents
45. Railroads
46. Shipping
47. Telegraphs, Telephones, and Radiotelegraphs
48. Territories and Insular Possessions
49. Transportation
50. War and National Defense

Figure 4-1 Titles of United States Code

Examples

35 U.S.C. § 101 (2006).
35 U.S.C.A. § 101 (West 1999).
35 U.S.C.S. § 101 (LexisNexis 2003).

State Statutes

Most of the 50 states and the District of Columbia refer to their statutes merely by title, chapter, and section numbers. Consult Table T.1 for the blueprint for each state jurisdiction (but remember to convert the typeface from large and small capitals to ordinary roman type).

Examples

Colo. Rev. Stat. Ann. § 7-101-101 (West 19xx).
Neb. Rev. Stat. Ann. § 13-201 (LexisNexis 19xx).
Ohio Rev. Code Ann. § 1701.01 (West 19xx).

Some states, however (generally the more populous ones, including California, Maryland, New York, and Texas), have so many statutes that they are categorized into separately named titles. Once again, follow the format provided for each state in Table T.1.

Examples

Cal. Evid. Code § 52 (West 19xx).
Md. Code Ann., Educ. § 16-148 (LexisNexis 19xx).
N.Y. Bus. Corp. Law § 694 (McKinney 19xx).

Miscellaneous Information

Year
According to *Bluebook* Rule 12.3.2, the year that is placed in the parenthetical is not the year the statute was enacted, but rather the year found on the

spine of the book, the year appearing on the title page, or the latest copyright year, in that order of preference.

Pocket Parts (Rule 12.3.1(e))
If you located your statute in a pocket part or softcover supplement to the main volume, indicate such in the parenthetical as follows:

15 U.S.C.A. § 1051 (West Supp. 2006).
11 U.S.C.S. § 301 (LexisNexis 2004 & Supp. 2009). (Note: Parenthetical indicates that the statute is located both in the hardback main volume as well as in the supplement or pocket part.)

Practice Tips

✓ Practitioners seldom include the parenthetical even though it is required by *The Bluebook*. Nearly all practitioners merely end their statutory citations after giving the section number of the statute, as in 35 U.S.C. § 601. Information in the parenthetical about the publisher of an unofficial set is particularly confusing due to merging of many legal publishing companies. To determine the publisher whose name should be inserted in a parenthetical, check the copyright page of the set of statutes you use.

✓ For many computers, you may create a section symbol or paragraph symbol by holding the "Alt" key and pressing "20" or "21," respectively, on the numeric keypad. Alternatively, select these symbols by accessing "Insert" and then "Symbol" from your toolbar menu.

Spacing (Rule 6.2(c))
Follow the spacing rules given in Chapter 3 and place adjacent single capitals next to each other with no spaces between them. Always place a space after a section symbol (§) just as you would hit the spacebar if you were typing the word "section."

Multiple Sections (Rule 3.3(b))
If you wish to direct the reader to several consecutive sections, give inclusive section numbers (separated by a hyphen) and use two section symbols with no spaces between them. If using a hyphen or dash would be ambiguous, use the word "to." Do not drop digits, because statutes can be numbered so oddly that on encountering the reference "42 U.S.C. §§ 101-04," a reader might think he or she was being directed to a statute called "section 101, subdivision 4," rather than being directed to read sections 101 through 104. Thus, the correct form is "42 U.S.C. §§ 101-104 (2006)" or "Ga. Code Ann. §§ 14-2-101 to 14-2-114 (1997). Similarly, do not use the expression "et seq." (meaning "and following") to direct a reader to several sections because it is too imprecise.

Section Symbol (Rules 6.2(c) and 12.10)
In "stand-alone" citations, use the section symbol § rather than the word "section" except for the first word of a sentence, which can never be a symbol. Thus, state "Section 107 provides a complete defense" rather than "§ 107 provides a complete defense." In textual sentences, spell out the word "section" except when referring to a provision in the United States Code. Thus, when referring to state statutes in textual sentences, you must use the word "section" and not the symbol for section (§). Do not abbreviate words in textual sentences. Thus, write "California Civil Code section 101 provides" and not "Cal. Civ. Code § 101 provides."

Odds and Ends
- The plural of § is §§.
- Cite to the official code whenever possible (Rule 12.2.1(a)).
- In citations to the Internal Revenue Code, the reference to the title ("26 U.S.C.") may be replaced with "I.R.C." Thus, "26 U.S.C. § 101 (2006)" may be replaced with "I.R.C. § 101 (2006)" (Rule 12.9.1).
- If a statute is known by a popular name, that name may be used with the citation if it would be helpful. For example, "Lanham Act § 44(e), 15 U.S.C. § 1126(e) (2006)" is correct (Rule 12.3.1).
- *The Bluebook* gives little guidance regarding the spacing for parenthetical portions of statutes but generally shows no spacing. Thus, cite "17 U.S.C. § 106(a)" rather than "17 U.S.C. § 106 (a)."

See the Appendix, Examples of State Cases and Statutes, for sample citations for all states and the District of Columbia.

Legislative Materials
(Rule 13; B5.1.6)

On occasion, legal writers discuss the history of certain statutes. For example, they might wish to compare the various versions of a bill, provide background about the intent of the statute according to its sponsor, or quote from floor debates. The material considered during the legislative process is called *legislative history* and may consist of versions of the bill, transcripts of committee hearings held to discuss the bill, committee reports issued after the hearings were held, or floor debates. Although there are other documents making up legislative history (joint resolutions, committee prints, and so forth), only the most commonly cited materials are discussed here.

Following are forms for federal legislative documents. Consult *The Bluebook* for information on citing state legislative documents. State legislative history is cited far less frequently than federal legislative history. Legislative history is not binding on a court. Like secondary authorities (discussed in Chapter 5), it is persuasive, not mandatory.

Bills (Rule 13.2)

Bills are introduced in either the House of Representatives or Senate during a congress. Each congress lasts two years and has two sessions, a first and a second. The first session always occurs in odd-numbered years, and the second session always occurs in even-numbered years. The first session of the 111th Congress began in January 2009. The 112th Congress begins in January 2011.

Cite bills as follows:

- Copyright Term Extension Act, H.R. 604, 105th Cong. § 3 (1998). This citation signals that the bill was the 604th piece of legislation introduced in the House of Representatives during the 105th Congress and that it was introduced in the second session (the year 1998 conveys this information). It directs the reader to section three of the bill.
- National Center for Social Work Research Act, S. 90, 109th Cong. § 1 (2005). This citation references the 90th bill introduced in the Senate in the first session of the 109th Congress and directs the reader to section one of the bill.

Once the bill has been signed by the president, it is a law and should be cited as a statute, namely to U.S.C., U.S.C.A., or U.S.C.S.

Committee Hearings (Rule 13.3)

After a bill is introduced, it is sent to a committee, which will then hold hearings regarding the proposed legislation. Various parties may testify in favor of or against the bill. Transcripts of the committee hearings are published, and citations include the following information: entire title as it appears on the cover of the transcript (treat this title as a book title and, thus, either underscore or italicize it), bill number, subcommittee or committee name (using abbreviations in Tables T.6, T.9, and T.10), particular Congress number, page of the transcript you wish the reader to review, and year of publication. If you wish, you may identify the witness who testified by using a parenthetical.

Cite committee hearings as follows:

> *The Motor Vehicle Safety Act of 2010: Hearings on S. 3302*
> *Before the S. Comm. on Commerce, Sci., & Transp.*,
> 111th Cong. 3 (2010) (statement of Sen. John D. Rockefeller IV).

Committee Reports (Rule 13.4)

After hearings are held, the committee issues a report giving its recommendations regarding the legislation. Citations to committee reports identify which house issued the report, number of the Congress connected by a hyphen to the number of the report, part or page to which the reader is directed, and year of publication.

Cite committee reports as follows:

- H.R. Rep. No. 105-42, at 16 (1998).
- S. Rep. No. 109-442, pt. 3, at 36 (2005).

Floor Debates (Rule 13.5)

A more or less verbatim transcript of debates occurring on the floor of the House of Representatives and Senate is printed in the *Congressional Record*, published each day Congress is in session. Initial pamphlets, called daily editions, are eventually replaced by hardbound permanent volumes. When citing to a daily edition, give the full date (using abbreviations shown in Table T.12). Cite to volume, set, page, and date. If desired, you may identify the speaker.

Cite floor debates as follows:

- 135 Cong. Rec. 1911 (1985) (statement of Sen. Strom Thurmond).
- 142 Cong. Rec. H401 (daily ed. Oct. 15, 1990) (statement of Rep. Frank Wolfe). (Note: The "H" preceding "401" indicates that the statements can be found in the House section of the daily edition.)

Uniform Acts (Rule 12.9.4; B5.1.3)

Uniform acts are drafted with the intent they will be adopted by all states. There are more than 250 uniform acts, the best known of which is the Uniform Commercial Code. Some states adopt the uniform act as drafted, whereas others make some changes to the act. A reference to a uniform law adopted by a state is cited just as any other statute from that state. West publishes a set entitled *Uniform Laws Annotated*, which publishes the uniform acts together with related information.

Examples

Uniform act:	U.C.C. § 2-316 (1977).
State version of act:	Cal. Com. Code § 2-316 (West 1998).
Uniform Laws Annotated:	Unif. P'ship Act § 29, 14 U.L.A. 164 (1998).

Court Rules (Rule 12.9.3; B5.1.3)

Cite court rules of evidence or procedure as follows:

Examples

Fed. R. Civ. P. 12(b)(3).
Fed. R. Crim. P. 40.
Fed. R. Evid. 210.
Sup. Ct. R. 33.
Cal. R. Ct. 1.44.

▮ **Constitutions** (Rule 11; B6)

U.S. Constitution

Cite the United States Constitution as follows:

Examples

U.S. Const. amend. XIV.
U.S. Const. art. I, § 8.

Remember to convert the large and small typeface you see in *The Bluebook* abbreviation of the word Constitution (CONST.) to ordinary roman type (Const.). View the inside front and back covers of *The Bluebook* and compare the different presentation styles for law review footnotes and court documents.

State Constitutions

Cite to state constitutions by using the appropriate abbreviations for the states provided in Table T.10 and setting up the citation in a manner similar to that used for the U.S. Constitution.

Examples

- Cal. Const. art. XXII.
- Nev. Const. art. II, § 4, cl. 6.

Practice Tip

✓ It might look odd to see a lowercase "a" used for "amend." and "art." when referring to constitutions in citations, but that is the rule. When you discuss a particular section of the U.S. Constitution in text, however, you will use uppercase letters, as follows: "The Fourth Amendment protects against unreasonable searches." Do not give any date if the constitutional provision is still in force.

Exercise for **Chapter 4**

Correct the following citations. You might need to supply missing information.

1. Tenth Amendment to the U.S. Constitution.

_____

2. Article 1, Section 8, clause three of the U.S. Constitution.

_____

3. Article 10 of the Nevada Constitution.

_____

4. House of Representatives bill number 4213, 111th Congress.

_____

5. Section 3 of Senate bill number 2711, 107th Congress.

_____

6. "The End to Discriminatory State Taxes for Automobile Renters Act of 2009." Hearing on H.R. 4175 before the House Committee on the Judiciary, statement of Representative John Conyers, Jr. (110th Congress)

_____

7. Statement of Senator Christopher J. Dodd, volume 155, pages 113-118 of the Congressional Record.

_____

8. Title 18, section 4422 of the United States Code.

_____

9. Title 42, section 1044 of the United States Code Annotated.

_____

10. Title 7, sections 1051 through 1059 of the United States Code Service. Assume this statute is located only in the pocket part of the set.

    _____

11. New York General Construction Law, section 1420.

    _____

12. Section 10-42-109 of the Montana Code Annotated.

    _____

13. Texas Government Code section 2422 Annotated.

    _____

14. Arizona Revised Statutes Annotated section 10-325.

    _____

15. Federal Rule of Civil Procedure 26(a).

    _____

16. Uniform Securities Act section 302.

    _____

17. Senate Report Number 230 from the 108th Congress, page 34.

    _____

5 Secondary Sources

Introduction

Sources other than cases, constitutions, statutes, treaties, and administrative regulations are called *secondary sources* and include books, articles, and encyclopedias. Legal writers prefer to cite to primary sources rather than secondary sources because primary sources are mandatory (meaning courts must follow relevant primary sources), whereas secondary sources are persuasive at best. Note that the examples given in *The Bluebook* for many of the secondary authorities show large and small capitals. As always, practitioners should convert this form to ordinary roman style.

Books and Treatises (Rule 15; B8)

Cite books, treatises, pamphlets, and other nonperiodical materials by including the following:

- Volume number (if it is a multivolume work).
- Author's name, set forth as the author himself or herself does, including any designation such as "Jr." or "IV." If there are two authors, list them both in the order given in the publication using an ampersand, as in "Leigh Peters & Sofia Bianco." If there are more than two authors, either use the first author's name followed by the signal

"et al." (meaning "and others") or list all of them. Follow the author's name with a comma.

- Title of book (underscored or italicized, depending on preference) given as it appears on the title page. Note that some titles include the author's name, as in *McCarthy on Trademarks and Unfair Competition*. Do not put any punctuation after a book title.
- Page, section, or paragraph, dropping repetitious digits for pages (Rule 3.2(a)), but not for sections or paragraphs (Rule 3.3(b) and (c)).
- Parenthetical information (including any editor or translator, edition of the book if there is more than one edition, and year of publication).

Examples

- 2 J. Thomas McCarthy, *McCarthy on Trademarks and Unfair Competition* § 4:13 (4th ed. 1998).
- 7 Samuel Williston, *Treatise on the Law of Contracts* § 901 (Walter H. Jaeger ed., 3d ed. 1964).
- Sandra Dolan, *Antitrust Law* § 4.06 (Anna Nelson trans., 4th ed. 1997).
- John Harris et al., *Indemnity Protection* ¶¶ 101-106 (1997).

▧ **Periodical Materials** (Rule 16; B9)

The publications that law schools periodically produce are generally called *law reviews*. Other periodical publications, such as the *Banking Law Journal*, are published to keep practitioners current in their chosen fields. Law reviews and law journals are frequently cited in court documents because they offer scholarly examinations of various legal topics.

A citation to a periodical generally includes the following:

- Author's full name as used by the author (follow the rules noted previously regarding multiple authors). If a note or comment (typically, a shorter piece) is written by a student, indicate such. (See example below.) Follow the author's name with a comma.
- Title of article written (underscored or italicized) and followed by a comma.

- Reference to the name of the periodical in which the article is published (cite to volume, set, and page, following the spacing and abbreviations shown in Table T.13).
- Year (given in parentheses).

Examples

David J. Hayes, Jr., *Due Process*, 41 Emory L.J. 164 (1995).
Janet R. Sanders, Note, *Juvenile Justice*, 77 Mass. L. Rev. 180 (1995).
Franklin Nelson & Taylor Luce, *The Common Law*, 13 J. Legal Educ. 245 (1990).

Dictionaries (Rule 15.8; B8)

There are several law dictionaries. They are cited according to the rules governing books and treatises. Give the name of the book, page on which the definition appears, and parenthetical with the edition (if other than the first edition) and year of publication.

Examples

Black's Law Dictionary 905 (9th ed. 2009).
Ballentine's Law Dictionary 54 (3d ed. 1969).

Encyclopedias (Rule 15.8; B8)

Encyclopedias provide an easy-to-read overview of hundreds of legal topics. There are two national sets (*Corpus Juris Secundum* and *American Jurisprudence, Second Series*) and about ten state-specific sets. Although the explanations of the law are articulate and easy to understand, because their approach is so elementary, encyclopedias are seldom cited in authoritative legal writing. Their citation form includes the following elements:

- Volume number
- Reference to name of set
- Topic name (underscored or italicized)

- Section number
- Year (in parentheses)

Examples

76 Am. Jur. 2d *Trademarks* § 63 (1994).
95 C.J.S. *Venue* § 4 (Supp. 1998). (Note: Parenthetical indicates that the information is found in the pocket part.)
14 Cal. Jur. 3d *Contracts* §§ 14-16 (1994).

▨ **Restatements** (Rule 12.9.5; B5.1.3)

The Restatements, the product of the American Law Institute, aim to restate the law of a particular topic in a clear and concise fashion. Comments and notes on the use of the Restatements follow each articulation of any legal principle. The Restatements are likely the most highly regarded of the secondary authorities and are frequently cited.

Cite to the name of the Restatement, section number, reference to comment (if applicable), and year of publication.

Examples

Restatement (Second) of Torts § 13 (1986).
Restatement (Second) of Contracts § 84 cmt. a (1986).

▨ **A.L.R. Annotations** (Rule 16.7.6)

Scholarly essays or annotations are published in *American Law Reports* on a variety of legal topics and are sufficiently respected that they may be cited in court documents and legal memoranda.

Citations include the following elements:

- Author's full name, followed by a comma
- The word "Annotation" followed by a comma

- Title of the work (underscored or italicized) followed by a comma
- Reference to volume, set, and page
- Year (in parentheses)

Examples

James W. Gray, Annotation, *Nuisance Theory*, 56 A.L.R.4th 145 (1990).
Lindsey Goodman, Annotation, *Defenses in Discrimination Cases*, 64 A.L.R. Fed. 909 (1996).

Practice Tip

✓ Never cite to a digest. Digests such as West's *Federal Practice Digest* or the *American Digest System* published by West are used as case finders. They help one find the law. They are neither primary nor secondary law themselves and, thus, can never be cited.

Exercise for Chapter 5

Correct the following citations. You might need to supply missing information.

1. Volume 64 of Am. Jur. 2d, section 104, discussing "trusts."

    _____

2. Volume 13 of Cal. Jur. 3d, section 11, discussing "battery."

    _____

3. Page 714 of the current edition of *Black's Law Dictionary*, defining the word "inchoate."

    _____

4. Volume 4 of the set of books titled "Wills, Trusts, and Estate Planning" by Ronald Cresswell, Sarah Patel Pacheco, and Patrick Pacheco, second edition, section 3:44.

---

5. Section 201 of the Restatement of Agency, Third.

---

6. Sections 101 through 104 of the Restatement of the Law, Second, Conflict of Laws, comment b.

---

7. Volume 2 of the fourth edition of "Insurance Law Handbook," written by Hillary R. Reynolds, paragraph 104.

---

8. A law review article authored by Sam Kamin in 2005, located in volume 46 and beginning at page 83 of the Boston College Law Review and entitled "The Private Is Public: The Relevance of Private Actors in Defining the Fourth Amendment."

---

9. Volume 104 of C.J.S., sections 104 through 110, discussing "Trespass."

---

10. A 2010 law review article authored by Stephen L. Logonsky, Jr., entitled "Restructuring Immigration Adjudication" and located at volume 59, page 1635, of the Duke Law Journal.

---

11. An annotation authored by Daniel H. White, entitled "Allowance of Attorneys' Fees Under the Clayton Act," published in volume 21 of A.L.R. Federal, beginning at page 750.

---

12. An annotation authored by Charles W. Benton at volume 43, page 149 of A.L.R. (5th) and entitled "Coverage Provisions in Automobile Liability Policies."

---

6 Administrative and Executive Materials, Electronic Databases, The Internet, Record Materials, and Court Documents

■ Administrative and Executive Materials (Rule 14 and Table T1.2)

In general, administrative materials consist of the rules, regulations, and other materials of federal administrative agencies (such as the Securities and Exchange Commission [SEC] or Federal Communications Commission [FCC]), adjudications, and various executive materials, such as presidential proclamations and executive orders.

Agency Law

Federal agencies have the power to make rules and regulations, which, if properly promulgated, have the effect of statutes. Moreover, the agencies have the power to issue decisions to enforce their rules. The rules and regulations first appear in a daily pamphlet called the *Federal Register*. The regulations are then codified or organized into 50 titles (highly similar to the arrangement of the *United States Code*) and produced in a set published yearly called the *Code of Federal Regulations*. If the agencies are called on to adjudicate a controversy, the decision may be published in various case reports.

Rules and Regulations (Rule 14.2)

Cite rules and regulations to the *Code of Federal Regulations* (C.F.R.) whenever possible, giving the title number, set name, section or part, and year. Giving the year is critical because a new set of C.F.R. is published each year. You may give the name of a rule or regulation if it is commonly cited that way or the name would be helpful.

Examples

- 18 C.F.R. § 701.254 (2009).
- 29 C.F.R. § 520.201 (2009).

Cite to the *Federal Register* only when the regulation has not yet been published in C.F.R., in which case give also any commonly used name of the regulation. Further, if the *Federal Register* indicates where the regulation will appear in C.F.R., give that information parenthetically. Citations to the *Federal Register* include the volume number, set, page number, and exact date.

Examples

- Agricultural Trigger Levels, 75 Fed. Reg. 25,200 (May 7, 2010).
- Egg Research and Promotion Order, 74 Fed. Reg. 49,342 (Sept. 28, 2009) (to be codified at 7 C.F.R. pt. 1250).

Practice Tip

✓ *The Bluebook* makes a distinction between a "year" and a "date." For example, a "year" is "2009." A "date," however, is a full date, such as "May 5, 2010." Use Table T.12 to determine the abbreviations for the months of the year.

Treasury Regulations (Table T1.2)

Treasury regulations are not cited to C.F.R. Use the following form: Treas. Reg. § 1.305-1 (1973).

Administrative Decisions (Rule 14.3 and Table T1.2)

Official Reporters

Decisions issued by various agencies may be published in the official reporters of the agency. Cite to the official reporter if the decision is found therein. Many of those reporters (and their correct abbreviations) are listed in Table T1.2 of *The Bluebook* (before the instructions given for each state). Cite to (and underscore or italicize) the full reported name of the first-listed private party (namely a party that is not an agency of the government) or the official subject-matter title, volume number, set name, page or paragraph, and year of decision (given in parentheses). As noted below, *The Bluebook* gives many examples for citing administrative agency materials in its new Table T1.2.

Examples

- *Network Solutions, Inc.*, 18 F.C.C.2d 909 (1998).
- *Stevens Textiles Co.*, 403 N.L.R.B. 120, 124 (1995).

Looseleaf Services (Rule 19)

Not every agency publishes its cases officially. A variety of private publishers (for example, Commerce Clearing House and Bureau of National Affairs) publish cases and other administrative materials unofficially in sets of binders called looseleaf services. For example, the *Business Franchise Guide* includes cases, statutes, administrative regulations, and a host of other information relating to franchise law. "Looseleaf" refers to the fact that as new material is released, old pages are taken out of the binders and the new pages are inserted. In some instances, the looseleaf binders are later replaced by bound volumes.

Generally, cite decisions in looseleaf services as follows: case name (underscored or italicized), volume, abbreviated title of set, publisher (in parentheses), reference to paragraph or section, court information and date (in parentheses, giving exact date for material found in a looseleaf service and the year only for material found in a bound volume). Older materials (especially older cases) or materials awaiting binding may be kept in semi-permanent "transfer binders." Table T.15 in *The Bluebook* provides a list of the most frequently cited looseleaf services, giving their proper abbreviations. If a set is not listed in Table T.15, use Table T.13 to locate appropriate abbreviations so you can construct a title.

Examples

In re Walmart Stores, Inc., 5 Bus. Franchise Guide (CCH) ¶ 42,201 (D.N.J. Aug. 12, 1995).

Davidson Co. v. Emory Inst., 24 Commc'ns Reg. (P & F) ¶ 9019 (S.D.N.Y. May 1, 1997).

In re Sav-All Drug Co., 6 Bankr. L. Rep. (CCH) ¶ 66,180 (Bankr. D. Or. Nov. 20, 1995).

In re Jacobs, [1994-1995 Transfer Binder] Fed. Sec. L. Rep. (CCH) ¶ 12,021 (M.D. Pa. July 10, 1995).

Administrative Agency Materials (Rule 14 and Table T1.2)

The new Nineteenth Edition of *The Bluebook* has greatly expanded its section on administrative agency materials. Table T1.2 now provides examples and information for several agencies, including the Department of Agriculture, Environmental Protection Agency, Federal Aviation Administration, and many more. For example, *The Bluebook* provides many useful examples for the following SEC materials: no-action letters, SEC releases, and various filings made with the SEC (including annual reports). (See Table T1.2.)

Similarly, recognizing the ever-increasing importance of intellectual property law, *The Bluebook* provides several examples for citing both filed and issued patents and registered and applied-for trademarks. Abbreviations are given for various publications of the U.S. Patent and Trademark Office in Tables T1.2, T.7, and T.15.

Practice Tip

✓ Although *The Bluebook* provides many forms and examples for administrative materials and services, practitioners often develop their own forms, typically using citation forms suggested or used by various agencies or tribunals. Rule 14 now provides that practitioners should always comply with an agency's preferences for citations and follow the agency's approach rather than that of *The Bluebook* if the two forms vary. If your office follows an agency's preferences for citations, ensure consistency in your office. Prepare your own mini citation manual and circulate it to your colleagues so everyone cites uniformly.

Presidential and Executive Materials (Table T1.2)

Presidents can issue proclamations (for action often having no legal effect, such as declaring March 2008 "American Red Cross Month") or executive orders (which have the effect of law until a court rules otherwise). Most presidential material is published in title 3 of C.F.R. If the material is also published in U.S.C. (or U.S.C.A. or U.S.C.S), give that citation also. If the presidential material is so recent it is not yet in C.F.R., cite to the *Federal Register* and give the exact date.

Examples

Proclamation No. 8109, 3 C.F.R. 180 (2007).
Proclamation No. 8465, 74 Fed. Reg. 67,801 (Dec. 15, 2009).
Exec. Order No. 13,452, 72 Fed. Reg. 67,827 (Nov. 28, 2007).
Exec. Order No. 13,393, 3 C.F.R. 690 (2005), *reprinted in* 3 U.S.C. § 343 (2006).

▌ **Lexis and Westlaw** (Rules 10.8.1, 18.3.1 and B4.1.4)

There are two major computerized legal research systems: LexisNexis ("Lexis") (owned by Reed Elsevier, Inc.) and Westlaw (owned by West, a Thomson Reuters business). Although there are some differences between the two systems, they are nearly equal in most respects. Many researchers enjoy using these computerized systems because they are easy to access and provide quick results. Of course, proficiency takes time and practice. The question then becomes, how does one cite to material located via Lexis or Westlaw?

The Nineteenth Edition of *The Bluebook* continues a prejudice against citing to the commercial electronic databases. *The Bluebook* (Rule 18) generally requires the use and citation of traditional printed sources when they are available. Nevertheless, *The Bluebook* acknowledges the reliability and authoritativeness of Lexis and Westlaw and prefers these electronic sources to the Internet. (See Rule 18.3.) Thus, cite a case to an electronic database such as Lexis or Westlaw only when the case has not been or will not be published in a conventional set of reporters. If a case is reported in conventional print materials, citation to Lexis or Westlaw would be inappropriate.

Similarly, for statutes, Rule 12.2.1 states that one should cite statutes to the official code. If that is unavailable, one may cite to an unofficial code, official session laws, privately published session laws, a commercial electronic database, looseleaf service, an Internet source, or newspaper, *in that order of preference*. Thus, citing statutes to Lexis or Westlaw can be done only when a federal statute is unavailable in U.S.C., U.S.C.A., U.S.C.S., or any session laws. Nevertheless, Rule 18 now provides that when an authenticated, official, or exact copy of a source is available online, citation can be made as if to the original print source. For example, because the new Federal Digital System (http://www.fdsys.gov) offers authenticated federal materials (including statutes and regulations), you may now cite to these without giving any URL information, as follows: 7 U.S.C. § 1081 (2006).

Why is citation to electronic databases frowned on when the databases have been in existence for years? Some experts speculate that citing to electronic databases makes retrieval difficult for some judges who might be unskilled in the use of the electronic databases. Over time, this will likely change. For now, however, the general rule is that one should cite cases or statutes to Lexis or Westlaw only when the authority is not available in conventional print form.

For cases found on Lexis or Westlaw, cite as follows: case name, docket number of case, database identifier, and court name and exact date parenthetically. If screen or page numbers have been assigned, indicate such with an asterisk before the relevant number. (See Rule 10.8.1.)

Examples

Cases   *Bowen Assoc. v. Capital Fin. Group*, No. 04-1765, 2006 U.S. App. LEXIS 12402, at *2 (4th Cir. Oct. 8, 2006).

	Green v. Taylor, No. 05-CV-120, 2007 WL 44102, at *1 (D.N.J. Feb. 10, 2007).
Short Forms	*Bowen*, 2006 U.S. App. LEXIS 12402, at *3.
	Green, 2007 WL 44102, at *2.

For statutes, cite to title, set, and section and then give parenthetically the name of the database and information relating to the currency of the database (rather than giving the year of the code). If the code is published unofficially, give the name of the publisher in the parentheses as well. (See Rule 12.5.)

Examples

Statutes	42 U.S.C. § 1204 (LEXIS through 2009 Sess.).
	Cal. Educ. Code § 155 (West, Westlaw through 2009 Sess.).
	S.D. Codified Laws § 21-103-19 (LEXIS through 2008 Legis. Sess.).

■ **The Internet** (Rule 18)

The Nineteenth Edition continues *The Bluebook*'s preference for conventional print materials over electronic sources. Rule 18.2 provides that traditional printed sources should be used and cited unless there is a digital copy of the source available that is authenticated, official, or an exact copy of the printed source.

At the time of the writing of this text, the federal government is migrating to a new electronic system, the Federal Digital System (usually called "FDsys," located at http://www.fdsys.gov), which is intended to provide "one-stop shopping" for nearly all legislative documents, including statutes, regulations, and presidential materials. The documents deposited into FDsys are "authentic," meaning their content is verified as authentic or official and thus one may readily cite to them as if citing to an original print source.

Similarly, many states have begun publishing their cases online and designating them as "official," meaning that you may cite to them as if citing to an original print source.

There are three basic rules for citing to the Internet:

- **Authenticated, official, or exact copies.** If an authenticated, official, or exact copy of a source can be located online, one may cite to it as if citing to the original print source. Authenticated copies are typically those that are marked with a logo verifying their accuracy. Materials that appear on FDsys show this logo of authenticity.

Example

17 C.F.R. § 229.302 (2010).

- **Internet source as parallel citation.** You may include a parallel citation to an Internet source with content that is identical to a traditional print source if the Internet citation will substantially improve access to the source cited. Give the traditional print source first, follow it with a comma, and introduce the Internet URL information with the italicized or underscored phrase *available at.*

Example

Dan L. Burk, *Biotechnology in the Federal Circuits: A Clockwork Lemon,* 46 Ariz. L. Rev. 441 (2004), *available at* http://www.law.arizona.edu/ Journals/ALR/ALR2004/vol463.htm.

- **Internet source as direct citation.** Many articles and materials exist only on the Internet; there is no print counterpart for them. *The Bluebook* refers to these materials as "direct" Internet citations. In such instances, follow *Bluebook* Rule 18.2.2, which provides specific direction on including author names, titles, dates, and the URL.

Example

David Healey, *A New Checklist for Patent Damages,* Fish News (Apr. 19, 2009), http://www.fr.com/A-New-Checklist-for-Patent-Damages-04-19-2010.

If direct Internet material is undated, indicate the date that the website was last visited, as follows: U.S. Copyright Office Home Page, http://www. copyright.gov (last visited Mar. 15, 2010).

Examples

Case published in print source but available on the Internet: *Feist Publ'ns Inc. v. Rural Tel. Serv. Co.*, 499 U.S. 340 (1991), *available at* http://caselaw.findlaw.com/scripts/getcase.pl?court=us&vol=499& invol.=340.

Statute published in print source but available on the Internet: 17 U.S.C. § 101 (2006), *available at* http://www4.law.cornell.edu/uscode/ 17/101.html.

Statute published in print source but authenticated version available on the Internet: 17 U.S.C. § 101 (2006).

Article available only on the Internet: Gregory L. Daley, *The Madrid Protocol*, United States Patent and Trademark Office (Apr. 14, 2009), http://www.uspto.gov/trademarks/law/madrid/index.jsp.

Practice Tips

✓ Typically, one only gives a date for direct Internet citations; however, if citing to "dynamic" material such as a blog or other site that is frequently updated, give the time as well in the date parenthetical, as follows: (June 21, 2010, 9:38 AM).

✓ *The Bluebook* prefers documents in PDF format to those in HTML format (Rule 18.2.2(f)).

✓ *The Bluebook* now gives some guidance on working with unwieldy URLs: If the URL is fairly straightforward, it should be cited as it appears in the address bar. If the URL is overly long or includes several nontextual characters (such as question marks and percentage signs), *The Bluebook* suggests that the root URL be provided and then an explanation of how to access the information should be provided parenthetically. Example: http://www.megalaw.com (select "State Laws," then select "California," then select "Search California Regulations," and then follow hyperlink).

■ Record Materials and Court Documents (Rule 10.8.3; B7; BT.1)

In many instances, legal writers wish to refer in a brief to other pleadings, motions, or materials that make up part of the court's record in a case. For example, a plaintiff might wish to draw the court's attention to an allegation made by the defendant in an answer to a complaint. *The Bluebook* offers only minimal guidance.

Follow these citation tips when citing to litigation documents filed in your case:

- Include the name of the document (abbreviated when appropriate), the pincite, and the date (if required).
- The pincite should be as precise as possible, including the page (not preceded by "p.") and line on which material appears in a deposition or trial transcript.
- The previous Eighteenth Edition of *The Bluebook* required that the reference be enclosed in parentheses. Many practitioners disliked this rule, and the new Nineteenth Edition of *The Bluebook* provides that the reference may optionally be enclosed in parentheses.
- You may string references together using semicolons to separate them from each other.
- Use the abbreviations shown in Table BT.1 of *The Bluebook*.
- Omit articles and prepositions from the title of a court document, unless confusion would result.
- You should use "at" when referring to pages in an appellate record. You are usually not required to use "at" before other pinpoint citations. Do not use "at" before a section or paragraph symbol.
- When citing court documents filed with the electronic case management system used by PACER (the federal government's system allowing public access to court documents and filings), add the electronic case file or "ECF" number to indicate a document that has been filed electronically, as follows: Pl.'s Mot. Dismiss 3, ECF No. 24.
- Do not abbreviate the title of a court document in a textual sentence.
- Ensure consistency in your citation form.
- Use the "hereinafter" form to establish an abbreviation of a long title described in text after you have cited the material in full the first time, as follows: "Juvenile Office Probation Sentencing Report" [hereinafter "Sentencing Report"].

Note: *The Bluebook* states that the word "hereinafter" and the shortened from appear in square brackets rather than in rounded parentheses, but practitioners usually use parentheses.

Example

Defendant has alleged that he revoked his acceptance of the contract. Def.'s Answer to Compl. ¶ 3. Nevertheless, Defendant has acknowledged that the purported revocation was mailed to Plaintiff only after Plaintiff had signed and delivered the contract. Def.'s Dep. 26:1-4, Jan. 31, 2009. As discussed in Plaintiff's Second Amended Motion for Summary Judgment [hereinafter "Motion"] and other witnesses have confirmed, Taylor Aff. ¶ 3, the mailing of the revocation was effected only after execution and delivery of the contract by Plaintiff. Gregson Decl. ¶ 14; Harrison Aff. ¶ 7; Franklin Admis. ¶ 9.

When citing to documents such as briefs filed in another case (for example, briefs filed in the U.S. Supreme Court case *Brown v. Board of Education*), follow *Bluebook* Rule 10.8.3.

Exercise for Chapter 6

Correct each citation. You might need to supply or create missing information. Assume citations are "stand-alone" citations.

1. "National Organic Program," volume 75 of the Federal Register, page 14500 (March 26, 2010), to be codified at 7 CFR part 205.

2. Title 37 of the Code of Federal Regulations, Section 263.3 (2009).

3. Section 4.34 of title 15 of the Code of Federal Regulations.

4. Executive Order 13,505 (assume the material is available in C.F.R.).

_____

5. Presidential Proclamation Number 8347 (assume the material is not available in C.F.R.).

_____

6. The registered trademark (Reg. No. 3,567,779) "Silent Running."

_____

7. The case _Black v. United States_, published at 550 U.S. 405 (but also available at the U.S. Supreme Court website).

_____

8. An October 24, 2009, article entitled "Coverage Under the Fair Labor Standards Act," written by Camille T. Taylor and available only at the Department of Labor website, http://www.dol.gov/whd/regs/compliance/whdfs14.htm.

_____

9. A Motion to Dismiss by all three defendants in a case (page 17).

_____

10. Paragraphs 24 through 29 of Defendant's Counterclaim.

_____

11. Page 230 of defendant Franklin S. Bailey's deposition, taken September 15, 2009.

_____

12. Exhibit B to Plaintiff's Complaint.

_____

13. _In re Willis Roof Consulting, Inc._, located in volume 4 of the Labor Law Reporter, paragraph 8410. This case was decided by the U.S. District Court for the Eastern District of Wisconsin in 2004.

_____

14. The unpublished case Reynolds v. Animal Care Clinics, Inc. decided in November 2009 by the U.S. District Court for the Middle District of Pennsylvania, Westlaw 34644.

---

15. The unpublished case Jacobson v. ADF, Inc., decided by the Ninth Circuit in January 2010, Lexis 22567.

7

Punctuation, Quotations, Omissions, Alterations, and Parentheticals

▓ Punctuation for Citations
(Rules 1.1 and 1.4; B2)

There are only three punctuation marks used after a citation is given: periods, commas, and semicolons. Use these marks as follows:

- Use a period to follow a citation when it supports or contradicts a previous declaratory sentence (Rule 1.1; B2).

Example

- Trademarks can be abandoned through nonuse. *Powell Mktg. Co. v. Hart Constr. Ltd.*, 482 U.S. 15 (1990). (Note: Such a citation ending with a period is a "stand-alone" citation, and thus, any of the more than 170 words in

Table T.6 in *The Bluebook* must be abbreviated in the case name, including the first word in the case name.)

- Use commas to set off a citation when the citation supports or contradicts only part of a sentence (Rule 1.1; B2).

Example

- Although trademarks can be abandoned by nonuse, *Powell Mktg. Co. v. Hart Constr. Ltd.*, 482 U.S. 15 (1990), evidence of nonuse must be clear and convincing, *Gen. Cas. Constr. Co. v. Kaye*, 483 U.S. 190 (1992).

  Note that abbreviations in the case name are used for the first citation in the example given above. Why? Although the case citation is not "standing alone" at the end of a sentence, it is not needed to make sense of the sentence. Thus, you may abbreviate words in the case name per Table T.6. Some attorneys, however, only abbreviate words in a case name if the citation is placed at the end of a sentence. Thus, follow your firm or office practice.

- Use a semicolon to separate citations from each other when more than one citation supports or contradicts a previous statement, namely, when the citations are placed in a "string." (See Rule 1.4.) Note that the string is often preceded by a signal such as *see*, *but see*, and so forth.

Practice Tip: String Citing

✓ In a citation string, the most helpful or authoritative citation should be placed first. Thereafter, the citations must be listed in the hierarchical order set forth in Rule 1.4, as follows:

- Statutes (first federal and then state statutes);
- Federal cases (starting with U.S. Supreme Court cases, then courts of appeal cases, and then district court cases, but treat all courts of appeal as one court and all district courts as one court, and within each group list newer cases before older ones); and

- State cases, listed alphabetically by state. (If there are several cases from the same state, list those from higher courts before those from lower courts, and within each grouping, list newer cases before older ones.)
- If you change to a different signal type, for example, listing a new string of cases introduced by the signal *But see*, rather than *see*, end your first string with a period. *Bluebook* Rule 1.3 at 56.

Example

- A general partnership agreement need not be in writing. *See Allen v. James Bus. Co.*, 433 F.2d 18 (8th Cir. 1990); *Daly v. Young*, 420 F.2d 26 (4th Cir. 1985); *Hardy v. Oakland Co.*, 401 N.E.2d 18 (Mass. 1990); *Malone v. Midwestern Realty Org.*, 414 N.E.2d 89 (Mass. App. Ct. 1996); *Powell v. Lyden Co.*, 412 N.E.2d 149 (Mass. App. Ct. 1995).

Quotations (Rule 5; B4.1.2 and B12)

Introduction: Pinpoint Cites (Rule 3.2 and B4.1.2)

When quoting from an authority you must give the specific page on or section at which the quotation appears. What if you are merely paraphrasing the authority rather than directly quoting from it? *The Bluebook* states that these pinpoint cites are critical for any cited proposition because they "provide the only means by which you can direct the reader to the exact page that contains the information or quotation on which you are relying for support." (*Bluebook*, B4.1.2 at 9.) Thus, give pinpoints for direct quotations and for paraphrased material.

Example

Copyrights are governed by federal law. *Wade v. Grayson*, 409 U.S. 14, 16 (1988); *Donoghue v. Cook*, 201 S.E.2d 409, 414 (Va. 1995).

The second page number is called a "pinpoint citation" or "pincite" because you are pinpointing for the reader exactly where to find material you are discussing. Occasionally, the second number is called a "jump citation," indicating you are asking the reader to jump to a certain page within a source.

The general practice is to always include the pinpoint citation, even if you are not directly quoting from a source. Why? It is the courteous approach, saving the reader from endlessly hunting through the authority trying to find the material you discuss. Moreover, if your research says what you claim it does, you should have no concern about allowing someone to verify your statements through the use of pinpoint citations. If a case has parallel citations, give the pinpoint citation for each, as follows: *Jones v. Smith*, 421 Ga. 106, 114, 729 S.E.2d 87, 94 (2004).

Shorter Quotations (Rule 5.1(b); B.12)

If your quotation is 49 words or fewer, do not indent it. Merely keep the quotation in the regular portion of your narrative. Use quotation marks (" ") to designate which material is being quoted, and *always* place commas and periods inside the quotation marks, even if your quote is only one word long. Other punctuation marks should be placed inside your quotation marks only if they are part of the material quoted. Should you count the words in a quote to determine its length? Yes, absolutely; you should always count the words.

Example

Courts have consistently held that although directors and officers of a corporation are not ordinarily liable for corporate obligations, this shield of limited liability will be pierced "when necessary to prevent fraud or injustice." *Carter v. Andrews Equip. Co.*, 482 U.S. 190, 194-95 (1995).

Lengthy Quotations (Rule 5.1(a); B12)

A quotation that is 50 words or longer should be indented 10 spaces left and right, single-spaced, and fully justified. Because the writing will appear as a chunk of words on the paper, this type of quotation is often referred to as a "block quotation." Do not use quotation marks for a block quotation. The fact that material is indented or blocked signals to the reader that it is a quotation.

Authors often place the citation for the quoted material within the indented block itself. This is incorrect. Only quoted material belongs in the block. The citation should be placed at the left margin on the first new line immediately following the block quotation (which appears two lines below the block quotation). If you then start a new paragraph, the citation might appear to be floating or hanging in space. Although odd-looking, this presentation is correct. Follow this format:

Xxxxxxxxxxxxxxxxxxxxxxxxxxxxxxxxxxxxxxxxxxxxxxxxxxxxxxxxxxxxxxx
xxxxxxxxxxxxxxxxxxxxxxxxxxxxxxxxxxxxxxxxxxxxxxxxxxxxxxxxxxxxxxx
xxxxxxxxxxxxxxxxxxxxxxxxxxxxxxxxxxxxxxxxxxxxxxxxxxxxxxxxxxxx

Lee v. Henry, 505 U.S. 6, 10 (1998).

Practice Tip

✓ You often see legal writers block-indenting quotes that are fewer than 50 words. Generally, this is done for stylistic reasons, so that the material is more dramatically presented to the reader. Many judges, however, are sticklers for *Bluebook* rules, so using a block for a short quotation merely for drama purposes might be disfavored.

Odds and Ends

- **Showing emphasis.** Do not use the expression "emphasis in original" if a word is italicized or otherwise emphasized in the original quotation. In legal writing, it is presumed that readers are sophisticated, and they will thus assume you have reproduced a quotation scrupulously. It is only when you change a quotation, perhaps by italicizing a word for emphasis, that you will indicate "emphasis added" (Rule 5.2). For example, the following is correct: The Court stated, "these limited liability partners are not personally liable for the acts of *misconduct* of their co-partners." *Randall v. Cox*, 500 U.S. 160, 165 (1994) (emphasis added). If you are underscoring rather than italicizing, use a solid unbroken line to show words you have emphasized.

- **Multiple pages.** If a quotation spans more than one page, give the inclusive page numbers, separated by a hyphen or dash, retaining the last two digits, but striking other repetitive digits, as follows: *Nelson v. Nelson*, 601 P.2d 920, 922-26 (Nev. 1995). (Rule 3.2(a)).

- **Quotation on first page.** If the material you discuss or quote appears on the first page of a source, repeat the page, as follows: Guy Talbot, *Bankruptcy Preferences*, 37 How. L.J. 18, 18 (1990). (Rule 3.2(a)).

- **Quotations within quotations.** In narrative text, if your quotation itself quotes from another source, switch from double quotation marks to single quotation marks to double quotation marks, and so forth (Rule 5.1(b)). In a block quotation, quotation marks should appear as they do in the original source (Rule 5.1(a)).

- **Nonconsecutive pages.** If referring to nonconsecutive pages, set the citation up as follows: *Amey v. Scalise*, 502 U.S. 14, 18, 22 (1997). (Rule 3.2(a)).

- **Repeated references.** If a point is repeatedly made throughout a source, omit the pinpoint citation and use the word "*passim*," which means "everywhere," as follows: *Marks v. Carson*, 506 U.S. 180 *passim* (1998). Note that there is no comma between the page number and *passim* (Rule 3.2(a)).

- **Paragraph structure.** If a quotation you are indenting is a new paragraph in the original source, indicate such by also indenting the first line of your block quotation. If your block quotation includes several paragraphs from the original material, a blank line should separate each paragraph from the next, and each paragraph within the block should be indented to mimic the paragraph structure of the original quote. Show the omission of an entire paragraph by four indented periods on a separate line (Rule 5.1(a)).

- **Line breaks.** *The Bluebook* gives no guidance on breaking a citation from one line to the next. Use good judgment, and break the citation in a way that is not confusing or visually distracting to the reader.

Example

    Xxxxxxxxxxxxxxxxxxxxxxxxxxxxxxxxxxxx
xxxxxxxxxxxxxxxxxxxxxxxxxxxxxxxxxxxxxxxx
xxxxxxxxxxxxxxxxxxxxxxxxxxxxxxxxxxxxxxxx.

    . . . .

    Xxxxxxxxxxxxxxxxxxxxxxxxxxxxxxxxxxxx
xxxxxxxxxxxxxxxxxxxxxxxxxxxxxxxxxxxxxxxx
xxxxxxxxxxxxxxxxxxxxxxxxxxxxxxxxxxxxxxxx.

- **Piggybacking.** If your quotation is originally from a case other than the one you are relying on, indicate such as follows: "Employers are vicariously liable for 'certain acts of their employees.'" *Edwards v. Lane*, 501 U.S. 294, 299 (1998) (quoting *O'Connor v. Schultz*, 450 U.S. 24, 27 (1990)). (Rules 5.2(e) and 10.6.2).
- **Justification.** *The Bluebook* (B12) states that block quotations are fully justified (meaning that the lines of typing end at the same place along the left and right margins). Check your firm's practice because some attorneys prefer a "ragged" right edge.

▒ **Omissions** (Rule 5.3)

It is acceptable to omit material from a quotation, as long as you indicate such. Use an *ellipsis* (three periods separated from each other by spaces that are preceded and followed by spaces) to show omitted material.

Example

"Punitive damages must be . . . based upon actual damages." *Harvey Ltd. v. Viacor, Inc.*, 451 U.S. 91, 97 (1990).

Follow these additional rules:

- To show that you omitted material at the end of a sentence, use four periods (three for the ellipsis and one to show the period at the end of the sentence), as follows: "A landlord must provide habitable premises to a tenant . . . ." Note that a space is placed before the first period.
- If you end a sentence and then omit matter at the beginning of the next sentence, set up the quotation as follows: "A corporation can be dissolved by the state. . . . [A]n involuntary dissolution involves a court proceeding." Note that there is no space after the word "state" and before the first period. Why? You are telling the reader that you did not omit any part of the first sentence. Thus, you retain its original punctuation.
- If you are merely quoting a phrase within a sentence, you do not need an ellipsis. Set up such a quotation as follows: The Court further

held that "sexual harassment is prohibited under Title VII" and is "a significant workplace problem."

- Never use an ellipsis to begin a quotation. Use a bracketed letter to show that language beginning a sentence has been omitted, as follows: "[I]t is axiomatic that damages are awarded for breach of contract." The placement of an uppercase "I" in the brackets shows that in the original quotation the "I" was a lowercase letter. This signals to the reader that the word "it" was not the first word of the sentence.

- It is acceptable to omit citations that appear in the middle of a quotation (generally because they clutter the quotation). Simply give your quotation and at the end include the phrase "citations omitted" in a parenthetical, as follows: "Consent is a defense to the tort of battery." *May v. Jeffers*, 681 P.2d 18, 25 (Cal. 1994) (citations omitted).

▨ **Alterations** (Rule 5.2)

An alteration is a minor change in a quote, such as changing a letter from upper- to lowercase (or vice versa), pluralizing or singularizing a word, changing a tense, correcting spelling, or adding a word. Use square brackets to show alterations.

Example

"[I]nfringement of trademarks can be shown by proof of [actual] confusion."

The use of the brackets in the preceding example tells the reader that in the original quotation the word "infringement" started with a lowercase "i" and that the word "actual" did not appear. Rather, the author inserted the word "actual" for purposes of style or readability.

Example

"The landlord[s] failed to act in accordance with contractual duties."

The use of the brackets in this example tells the reader that in the original quotation the word "landlord" was singular. Here, the author wants to pluralize the word for purposes of style. An empty bracket in a word, for example, "action[ ]," tells the reader that in the original quotation there was another letter in the word (clearly, the word was "actions").

▨ **Parentheticals** (Rules 1.5, 10.6, and 10.7; B4.1.5; B11)

Legal writers often use parenthetical expressions to convey certain information (other than dates). Generally parentheticals fall into two categories.

- **Weight of authority.** Some parentheticals tell the reader something about the strength or weakness of the citation. Some of the more frequently used parentheticals to show weight of authority are as follows: en banc; 5-4 decision; mem. (for memorandum decisions, namely those in which a court issues a holding but gives either no or very little opinion); per curiam (meaning "by the court," indicating an opinion in which no particular author is identified); and identifications of concurring, dissenting, and plurality opinions.

Examples

- The Court upheld the doctrine of equivalents. *Carley v. Bennett*, 404 U.S. 16, 19-21 (1985) (9-0 decision).
- The endorsement test should be used in First Amendment cases examining separation of church and state. *Sherman v. Carlson*, 410 U.S. 610, 646 (1987) (O'Connor, J., dissenting).
  Note: Readers will always assume you are relying on the majority opinion. Thus, if you rely on a plurality, dissenting, or concurring opinion, you must indicate such by the use of a parenthetical.

- **Explanatory parentheticals.** Explanatory parentheticals are those that provide some explanation about the case. They should be given after parentheticals that indicate the weight of authority but before any subsequent history. Note that the expression in the parenthetical usually begins with a present participle (a verb ending in "-ing" such as "holding" or "rejecting"). They may also consist of an entire quoted sentence or a short statement. (B11)

Remember that we have already discussed certain parenthetical expressions, namely the expressions "citations omitted," used when you wish to delete citations from the middle of your quotation and "piggybacking," used to indicate that your case relied on or quoted from an earlier case.

Examples

- *Lowell v. Lynn*, 689 F.2d 191, 194-97 (D.C. Cir. 1990) (3-0 decision) (holding that trademarks can be diluted either by blurring or tarnishment).
- *Miller v. Malone Dev. Fed'n*, 13 F. Supp. 2d 101, 104 (C.D. Cal. 1998) (rejecting the doctrine of reverse equivalents), *aff'd*, 40 F.3d 16 (9th Cir. 1999).
- *Raymond v. Timmons*, 489 U.S. 16, 18 (1995) (5-4 decision) (quoting *Jamison v. Woods*, 456 U.S. 890, 895 (1990)).

Practice Tips

✓ Parenthetical information should appear in the following order:

- Weight of authority parentheticals (such as "6-3 decision");
- "Piggybacking" parentheticals (namely, those starting with the words "quoting" or "citing"); and
- Explanatory parentheticals (those that explain something about the case, usually starting with phrases such as a "noting that" or "holding that" or similar "-ing" words.)

✓ Subsequent history appears after any explanatory parenthetical. See Rule 1.5(b) for a full listing for the order of parentheticals.

✓ The "J." used to refer to an author of a dissent or concurring opinion stands for "Judge" or "Justice." It does not stand for the writer's first name. Always use "J." (See Table T.11.)

✓ If what is placed in the parentheses is a full sentence, it should begin with a capital letter and end with a period.

Exercise for **Chapter 7**

Correct the following statements and citations. There might be more than one thing wrong with each citation, and you might need to create missing information. Unless otherwise directed, assume that state court cases are being cited in internal office memoranda.

1. In United States of America versus Bailey, 444 U.S. 394, 409-410, the Court noted that "there is no federal statute defining ... the elements of the duress defense."

    _____

    _____

    _____

2. Show that the case in question 1 was decided by a five to four decision and that the quotation appeared on the first page of the case.

    _____

    _____

    _____

3. "A district court must retain the absolute control and power to insist upon some specificity in pleading before allowing a potentially massive factual controversy to proceed." *Bell Atlantic Corp. v. Twombly*, 550 U.S. 544, 546-548 (2007).

    a. Fix any errors in the citation.

    _____

    _____

b. Show that the foregoing quotation appears on page 558.

_____

_____

c. Omit the phrase "absolute control and" from the quotation and elim-
    inate the words "before allowing a potentially massive factual con-
    troversy to proceed."

_____

_____

_____

d. Show how to emphasize the word "absolute" in the foregoing
    quotation.

_____

_____

e. Indicate that the quotation is from a dissent by Justice Stevens.

_____

_____

f. Change the first three words ("A district court") to "District courts."

_____

_____

4. "A grant of summary judgment is always reviewed de novo." Reliance
    Insurance Company v. McGrath, 671 Federal Supplement, Second Series
    at page 669, decided by the Northern District of California in 1997.
    In a single citation, show all of the following:
    a. Show that the case was decided by a 3-0 decision.
    b. Show that the case was affirmed by the Ninth Circuit the next year in
        volume 110 of the Federal Reporter, Third Series, at page 102.
    c. Show that you emphasized the word "always."

_____

_____

_____

_____

5. Fix any errors in the following string citation.

Equitable estoppel may apply where there has been an admission, state-ment, or act that has been justifiably relied upon to the detriment of another party. *Keller v. Prince George's County*, 827 F.2d 952, 964 (4th Cir. 1987), which cited Patsy v. Board of Regents, 457 U.S. 496, 515 (1982). Avery v. County of Burke, 660 F.2d 111, 114, 115 (4th Cir. 1981). *Theilmann v. Rutland Hospital, Inc.*, 825 F.2d 853, 855 (2d Cir. 1987); *Allen v. Bullis*, 124 P.3rd 190, 198 (Wash. Ct. App. 2001). *Estate of Lyons v. Sorenson*, 83 Wash.2d 105, 108, 515 P.2d 1293 (1973); *Young v. Estate of Snell*, 948 P.2d 1291 (Wash. 1997); *People v. Monterroso* 101 P.3d 956 (Cal. 2004).

_____

_____

_____

_____

_____

_____

_____

8 Short Forms, Signals, Related Authority, and Capitalization

■ **Short Forms** (Rule 4; Bluepages *passim*)

Citation form is difficult and painstaking. Thus, any time you can avoid giving a citation in full, you should. In general, once a citation is given in full, you may later use a "short form" of it. *The Bluebook* states that short forms may be used if it will be clear to the reader what is being referenced, the earlier full citation is in the same general discussion, and the reader can quickly locate the earlier full citation. Use of the short forms is optional, not mandatory, but most legal professionals use short forms. Do not give a short form until you have given the full citation.

Id. (Rule 4.1)

Id. is a signal meaning "in the same place" that instructs a reader to return to the immediately preceding citation, no matter what it is. Follow these five rules:

- *Id.* can be used to send a reader to any preceding legal authority. It cannot, however, be used to direct a reader to an internal cross-reference, such as an earlier section in your brief.

91

- The word *id.* is itself an abbreviation. Thus, it is always followed by a period.
- *Id.* is a foreign word. Thus, it should be italicized or underscored. (Italicize or underscore the period, as follows: *id.* or id.)
- *Id.* can appear by itself, in which case it starts with a capital letter, or it can appear as a clause in the middle of a sentence, in which case it begins with a lowercase letter.
- The use of *id.* by itself tells the reader to go back to the immediately preceding authority. If you wish to send the reader to a different page, section, or paragraph within that authority, indicate that as shown in the following example.

Example

- The Court flatly announced its support for the doctrine of joint and several liability. *Farley v. Dayton-Hudson, Inc.,* 520 U.S. 16, 19 (1998). Thus, liability may be imposed upon any partner in a general partnership. *Id.* If, however, creditors know a partner has no authority to do a particular act, other partners may be insulated from liability. *Id.* at 26.

Three additional tips on using *id.* are:

- The use of *id.* for a case with a parallel citation does not significantly shorten the citation when you send the reader to a different page. For example, if the first citation is *Kenney v. Plaisance,* 231 Va. 16, 18, 204 S.E.2d 424, 427 (1990), the *id.* form is as follows: *Id.* at 21, 204 S.E.2d at 430. *Id.* only takes the place of the official citation.
- You cannot use *id.* when the preceding citation includes more than one source. For example, if a string citation or footnote contains more than one citation, you cannot use *id.* (otherwise, the reader will not know to which of the preceding references the *id.* signal refers).
- Note that per Rule 3.3, you cannot use the word "at" before a section sign (§) or a paragraph symbol (¶).

Examples

First reference (case page):   *Wilson v. Preston,* 490 U.S. 14, 16 (1995).
Second reference (case page):   *Id.* at 21.

Third reference (case page): *Id.* at 24.

First reference (section sign): Edward Riley, *Patent Practice* § 101 (1995).

Second reference (section sign): *Id.* § 104. (Note: The word "at" is not used.)

Supra (Rule 4.2; B8.2)

Supra means "above" and is a signal used to send a reader to a preceding citation, but not an immediately preceding citation. Note, however, that *supra* cannot be used to refer to primary authorities such as cases, statutes, regulations, constitutions, or to Restatements, or many legislative materials. It is thus used nearly exclusively to refer to previously cited books, law review and journal articles, and other secondary authorities. It must appear with the name of an author or some other identifying word rather than merely by itself, as does *id*. Although *The Bluebook* is clear that *supra* may not be used as a short form for cases or other primary authorities, some practitioners ignore this rule. If a comma follows *supra*, do not italicize (or underscore) the comma.

Examples

Page one of brief: Eve Jones, *Due Process*, 36 N.C. L. Rev. 401, 408 (1995).

Page two of brief: *Li v. Li*, 482 U.S. 120, 126 (1985).

Page three of brief: Jones, *supra.* or Jones, *supra,* at 412.

Internal Cross-References (Rule 3.5)

Note that in the preceding example, the use of *supra* directs the reader to the page within Eve Jones's article but does not tell the reader where exactly in your brief the reader will find your original citation to Eve Jones's article. Should you include this information? *The Bluebook* does not require that you tell the reader where in your document he or she will locate the previous citation but states you may do so (Rule 3.5). Use the following form: "Jones, *supra* p. 2, at 414" (directing the reader to page two of your document and then instructing the reader to review page 414 of Eve Jones's article). Note that "p." and "pp." are used only to direct a reader to pages within your document and not to pages within the published authority you are discussing.

When is *supra* followed by a comma? *Supra* is followed by a comma when you are directing the reader to the page or section of the previously cited published authority, as in "Jones, *supra*, at 414." When you are directing the reader to a previous page within your document — such as "Jones, *supra* p. 2, at 414." — there is no comma following the signal.

On some occasions, a brief might use the signal *infra*, meaning "below," to send a reader to a later discussion in the document, as in, "The issue of reckless conduct is discussed in Section IV, *infra*." The rules governing *supra* apply equally to *infra*. It is also likely that you will encounter *infra* in indexes or texts. Thus, in Chapter 7 of a textbook you might be informed, "For a further discussion of this topic, see *infra* Chapter 10."

Use of "Hereinafter" (Rule 4.2(b))

Use "hereinafter" to abbreviate the name of a secondary authority (or a legislative hearing) that is long and cumbersome. Enclose the form in brackets. (Note that practitioners tend to use rounded parentheses rather than square brackets.) For example, use the following format: *Sonny Bono Copyright Term Extension Act: Hearings on S. 562 Before the H. Comm. on Energy & Commerce*, 105th Cong. 121 (1997) [hereinafter *Copyright Hearings*]. Note two critical items: First, as with *supra* and *infra*, you should not use "hereinafter" to refer to primary authorities (meaning you cannot use it as a shorthand signal for a case, statute, regulation, or constitution); and second, once you establish the shorthand abbreviation, you must consistently use it thereafter. Thus, any later reference to the preceding hearings must consistently be called *Copyright Hearings*. This later shortened reference will usually appear with *supra* as in the following: *Copyright Hearings, supra*.

Short Forms for Cases (Rule 10.9; B4.2)

What if you cite a case on page two of your brief, then you cite a book on page three, and you wish to cite the case again on page four? You cannot use *id.* because that signal will send the reader to the book that is the immediately preceding citation. You cannot use *supra* because that signal cannot be used to send a reader to a case. Assume the case you cited on page one is *Gibbs v. Li*, 492 U.S. 420, 426 (1992). There are three alternatives you may use.

- Option 1 (B4.2):   *Gibbs*, 492 U.S. at 428.
- Option 2 (B4.2):   492 U.S. at 428.

- Option 3 (Rule 10.9(c)):　　Use *"Gibbs,"* with no further citation, if you have cited *Gibbs* in the same general discussion, for example, "In *Gibbs,* the Court also addressed the issue . . . ."

You may choose the most appropriate option as long as the reader will have no doubt as to which case you are discussing. Thus, use options 2 and 3 only when you have been discussing the authority with such frequency that the reader will have no doubt about the case to which the citation refers and no trouble locating the earlier citation. With regard to option 3, *The Bluebook* does not define the meaning of the term "same general discussion." Use common sense, realizing that if you have not mentioned the *Gibbs* case in several pages, the reader might have difficulty remembering or finding the citation if you only refer to it by name. In such instances, help the reader by giving more rather than less information.

For cases with parallel citations, the short forms are not particularly short. For example, if your first citation was *Young v. Barwich,* 231 Va. 106, 108, 320 S.E.2d 114, 118 (1990), the later citation (assuming you cannot use *id.* because there is an intervening citation) is one of the following:

- *Young,* 231 Va. at 110, 320 S.E.2d at 120.
- 231 Va. at 110, 320 S.E.2d at 120.
- "In *Young,* the court also noted . . . ."

Practice Tip

✓ Although you should generally use the plaintiff's name when sending a reader back to a case, use the defendant's name if the plaintiff's name is a governmental or other common litigant such as "State" or "United States." Thus, a later reference to *United States v. Bailey,* 444 U.S. 394, 409 (1980) would be *Bailey,* 444 U.S. at 415.

Short Forms for Other Authorities

Use the following short forms for authorities other than cases:

- For statutes and regulations, the first citation should be complete. Later references may use any form that clearly identifies the material (B5.2). Thus, the first reference to a statute would be 17 U.S.C.A. § 101

(West 2006), whereas the later reference could be *id.*, 17 U.S.C.A.
§ 101, or § 101 (Rule 12.10; B5.2).

- For constitutions, do not use any short form other than *id.*
  (Rule 11; B6).
- For books, law reviews, and other secondary authorities, use *id.* to
  send the reader to an immediately preceding authority and *supra*
  (with author's name or other identifying information) to send a
  reader to a source that is not immediately preceding, as in "McCarthy,
  supra, § 14:20." (Rule 4.2; B8.2).

Practice Tips

✓ The words or abbreviations *id., supra,* and *infra* are always
  underscored or italicized, but "hereinafter" is not.
✓ When using short forms for cases, do not include any
  subsequent history.
✓ Some practitioners follow *Bluebook* rules for law review footnotes for the use of short forms, meaning that they only use a
  short form if the full citation can be found in one of the preceding five footnotes or references (Rule 10.9). This rule
  relates solely to law review footnotes and is not required
  for practitioners.

■ Signals (Rule 1.2; B3)

Authorities cited by legal writers might support or contradict statements
made by the writer or might merely provide background material. Citation
signals allow a writer to indicate such without having to explain in full the
specific manner in which the cited authority is used. Signals are thus a form
of code, instantly conveying information to a reader. Unfortunately,
cracking the code is difficult and uncertain due to the vague manner in
which *The Bluebook* directs a writer as to the use of the signals.

Signals are divided into four categories: those that show support, one
that suggests a useful comparison, those that indicate contradiction, and
one that indicates background material. They precede case names or other
authorities as follows: *See Brown v. Casey*, 500 U.S. 490, 495-98 (1998). If no
signal is used before a citation, the reader should assume that the cited
authority directly states the proposition, identifies the source of a quotation,

or identifies an authority mentioned in the preceding text. The signal *see* indicates that the cited authority clearly supports the principle stated by the author. *See* is used instead of "no signal" when the proposition is not directly stated by the cited authority but obviously follows from it.

The situation is complicated by the fact that over the years, the use of certain signals has shifted. For example, until the Sixteenth Edition, the signal *contra* informed a reader that the cited authority directly stated the contrary of the proposition. The signal *contra* did not exist in the Sixteenth Edition but reappeared in the Seventeenth Edition. Thus, analyzing briefs, documents, and articles written prior to late 2000 (when the Seventeenth Edition was issued) results in a different interpretation of some signals. (See Figure 8-1 for a chart showing changes in signals.) The Eighteenth and Nineteenth Editions of *The Bluebook* are the same as the Seventeenth Edition with regard to the meaning and use of signals.

What do these confusing rules and signals mean to practitioners? Consider the following tips:

- Review the signals set forth in Rule 1.2, and recognize that distinctions between some signals are nearly indecipherable.
- Use no signal when you are quoting or when the cited authority directly states the proposition.
- Use *see* when your authority clearly supports the statement you are making but requires an inferential step between the authority cited and the proposition it supports.
- When totally confused, consider using no signal and then discussing parenthetically the meaning of the authority cited, for example: *Parks v. Carter*, 432 P.2d 18, 20 (Cal. 1994) (holding that . . . .).

Presentation of Signals

Perhaps even more difficult than learning what *The Bluebook*'s signals mean is learning how to present the signals. Follow these guides:

- Capitalize the signal only if it begins a sentence. Otherwise, use a lowercase letter.
- Italicize or underscore signals when they are used in citation sentences or clauses. If the signal is two words, use a solid unbroken line, for example: <u>See generally</u> Paul S. Kaye, <u>Blue Sky Law</u>, 201 Mo. L. Rev. 118, 120 (1988).
- When underscoring, separate the signal from an authority that is also underscored with a broken line, as follows: <u>See</u> <u>Ford v. Hazard</u>, 689 F.2d 118, 134 (9th Cir. 1990).

	Fifteenth Edition	Sixteenth Edition	Seventeenth Edition	Eighteenth and Nineteenth Editions
[No signal]	Citation clearly states the proposition, identifies the source of a quotation, or identifies an authority referred to in text.	Citation identifies the source of a quotation or identifies an authority referred to in text.	Citation directly states the proposition, identifies the source of a quotation, or identifies an authority referred to in text.	Same as Seventeenth Edition.
See	Citation clearly supports the proposition.	Citation directly states or clearly supports the proposition.	Citation clearly supports the proposition.	Same as Seventeenth Edition.
Contra	Citation directly states the contrary of the proposition.	*Contra* signal did not exist in the Sixteenth Edition	Citation directly states the contrary of the proposition.	Same as Seventeenth Edition.

Figure 8-1 Chart Showing Changes in *Bluebook* Signals

- When combining the signal *see* with another signal such as *e.g.* (to indicate that other authorities also clearly support the proposition, but giving their citations would not be particularly helpful), follow the word *see* with a comma, as follows: *See, e.g., Allen v. Riley*, 610 P.2d 118 (Or. 1997).
- Do not italicize or underscore the signal if you use the signal as an ordinary verb in a sentence rather than as a shorthand instruction to the reader. Thus, the following is correct: "For a general discussion of deeds of trust, see 78 C.J.S. *Deeds and Conveyances* § 48 (1994)."
- When using a variety of signals within a "string," note that Rule 1.3 imposes a hierarchy on their presentation, meaning they should be listed in the order in which they are presented in *The Bluebook* (namely, supporting signals, comparative signal, contradictory ones, and background signal). If there are two supporting signals, they should be separated from each other by semicolons. If those two signals are followed by a signal indicating contradiction, a new sentence should be started to show the new type of signal. An example is provided in Rule 1.3 of *The Bluebook*.
- Authorities within each signal are separated from each other by semicolons and presented in the order given in Rule 1.4 (statutes listed before cases, federal cases listed before state cases, cases from higher courts listed before cases from lower courts, and so forth).

Conclusion

The use of citation signals is frustrating even for the most practiced writers. Continually and carefully review their meanings. Because the signals can be so confusing, consider adding a parenthetical after your citation to clarify for the reader why your citation is given. Reread Rule 1.2 several times so you can quickly and immediately convey to a reader the import of the authorities you cite. In the long run, mastering the citation signals will save you much time.

▓ **Related Authority** (Rule 1.6)

On occasion, writers might wish to direct a reader to an authority related to or that discusses or quotes the specific authority cited. Such direction is accomplished through an italicized (or underscored) phrase that does not appear in parentheses. Commonly used directions include *quoted in, construed in, available at,* and *questioned in.* Use the following format: Hatch Act § 1, 36 U.S.C. § 50 (2006), *construed in James v. NRCC,* 520 U.S. 118, 126-27 (2007). If underscoring, use a solid unbroken line for the phrase, as follows: Linda Allen, Treble Damages in Antitrust Cases, 6 Duke L.J. 203 (1994), reprinted in Philip Hendrix, The Law of Antitrust 45 (3d ed. 1999).

Note that a parenthetical explanation that follows an authority and the first word of which ends with the suffix "-ing" (such as "quoting," "citing," or "construing") is not italicized or underscored, although phrases that introduce related authority (such as *quoted in* or *reprinted in*) are underscored or italicized. Thus, the following is correct: *Monument Sav. Bank v. Tyson Fed'n,* 504 U.S. 106, 109 (1997) (quoting *Draper v. Farrell,* 501 U.S. 19, 22 (1995)).

▓ **Capitalization** (Rule 8; B7.3)

The Bluebook includes a number of rules relating to the capitalization of certain words. The most significant rules are as follows:

- Capitalize the "C" in Court:
  - ➤ Whenever you refer to the U.S. Supreme Court.
  - ➤ When referring to the court to which you are addressing a document or request (for example, always state "Plaintiff respectfully urges this Court to grant her Motion for Summary Judgment").
  - ➤ When naming a specific court in full (as in the following: "The Eighth Circuit Court of Appeals clearly held that . . . .").

- Do not capitalize the "c" in "court" when you are discussing a court (other than the U.S. Supreme Court) in a general manner, such as follows: "The court in *Taylor* also held . . . .").

- Capitalize party designations such as "Plaintiff," "Petitioner," or "Defendant" when you refer to parties in the matter that is the subject of your document but not when they refer to parties in other actions, as follows: "The Defendant has asserted in his Answer that this action is barred by the statute of limitations. Plaintiff submits that Defendant has misinterpreted the position of the defendant in *Anderson*."

- Capitalize the first letter in each significant word in the title of a court document, such as the following: "In Plaintiff's Motion to Compel Answers to Interrogatories, Plaintiff argues that . . . ."

- Capitalize proper nouns referring to the Constitution or specific acts, such as "First Amendment," "Bill of Rights," and "Gold Clause Act."

- Capitalize "circuit" only when referring to a particular circuit by name or number, such as in the following statement: "The Ninth Circuit ruled that . . . ."

- Capitalize the "J" in justice or judge when giving the name of a specific jurist or when referring to any U.S. Supreme Court Justice, as in "Justice Breyer" or "the Justice stated . . . ."

- Capitalize the word "state" when it is part of the full title of a state, as in "the State of Ohio."

- Capitalize words in a heading or title in your brief, including the first word and any word that follows a colon. Do not capitalize articles (a, an, and the), conjunctions (for, and, nor, but, or, yet, so), or prepositions that have four or fewer letters (unless they begin a heading or follow a colon).

Practice Tips

✓ Although most writers have been taught to spell out the numbers one through nine and use figures for the numbers 10 and larger, *The Bluebook* position is quite different: *The Bluebook* instructs one to spell out the numbers zero to ninety-nine (Rule 6.2).

   Additionally, *The Bluebook* states that one should use commas in numbers only when the number contains five or more digits (Rule 6.2). Thus, *The Bluebook* provides that one write, "There are 9876 pages in the transcript." Most writers would prefer to write, "There are 9,876 pages in the transcript."

✓ *The Bluebook*'s Rule 8 states that when its capitalization rules do not address a particular issue, one should refer to a style manual such as the *Government Printing Office Style Manual*. This GPO *Style Manual* is an excellent source of information about writing, grammar, and usage. It is available online at http://www.gpoaccess.gov/stylemanual/index.html.

Exercise for Chapter 8

A. Correct the following. Assume that each number to the left of a question refers to a page within a brief being submitted to a court in your state and that there are no intervening citations between questions. If alternative forms of citation are acceptable, give all. Assume the citations are "stand-alone" citations.

1. *Scheuer v. Rhodes*, 416 United States Reports 232, 236, a 1974 case.

_____

_____

2. Refer to page 340 of the *Scheuer* case.

_____

_____

3. A 2009 law review article by Richard A. Nagareda titled "Class Certification in the Age of Aggregate Proof," and published at volume 84, page 97 of the New York University Law Review, with a pincite of page 131.

_____

_____

4. Refer to page 139 of the law review article.

_____

_____

5. Volume 4 of the treatise *The Business Judgment Rule*, third edition, 2008, section 12:20, written by Alexander F. Drummond.

_____

_____

6. Refer to section 12:45 of the previous treatise.

_____

_____

7. Refer to page 150 of the law review article.

_____

_____

8. Refer to page 342 of the *Scheuer* case.

_____

_____

9. Refer to section 12:49 of the treatise by Alexander F. Drummond.

_____

_____

B. Correct the following and describe the meaning of any signal used.

1. See also Asahi Glass Co. v. Pentech Pharmaceuticals, Inc., 289 Federal Supplement, Second Series 986, 995 (Northern District Illinois).

_____

_____

2. Cf. DM Research, Inc. v. College of American Pathologists, 170 F. 3rd 53, 56, (First Circuit 1999).

_____

_____

3. For additional discussion of this topic, see 1 Wayne R. LaFave, Substantive Criminal Law §5.1 (second edition 2003).

_____

_____

C. Correct the following statements made in a brief submitted to a court.

The plaintiff in this case has vigorously argued that she has been deprived of her right under the seventh amendment to the USA constitution to a fair trial. The facts, however, show that the plaintiff and defendant entered into a valid agreement to arbitrate any claims they may have had against each other. In fact, plaintiff's prior motion for summary judgment (paragraphs 34 through 40) acknowledges the existence of the arbitration agreement. Moreover, as noted by justice Sandra Day O'Connor, "[a]n agreement to arbitrate is as binding as any other agreement." Morrissette v. United States, 447 U.S. 16, 18 (2007), which was quoted in volume 8 of the treatise titled "Newberg on Class Actions," and authored by William B. Rubenstein, et al., Section 24:115. The present case is quite unlike *Morrissette*, in which the court found the plaintiff had never agreed to arbitration.

_____

_____

_____

_____

_____

_____

_____

_____

_____

_____

9 Putting It Together

The Table of Authorities

Many documents need (and court rules might require) a table of the authorities cited in the document. The table is presented at or near the beginning of the document or brief. A table of authorities lists each authority cited in a brief (whether in text or footnotes) together with a reference to the page or pages of the document on which each appears so that readers can readily locate a discussion of specific cases or other authorities. Although *The Bluebook* gives hundreds of pages of information about isolated citations, it provides no direction whatsoever as to setting up a table of authorities. Thus, comply with court rules (if they exist) or your firm or office practices (if they exist). Failing any direction, consider the following:

- Although many word processing programs and Lexis's FullAuthority and West's CiteAdvisor will automatically extract citations from your document and create a table of authorities, some individuals still prefer to use the "old-fashioned" approach: listing each authority in a separate document or on an index card and then "shuffling" them until they are in the right order.
- Citations that appear in a table of authorities are literally "stand-alone" citations (in that they appear by themselves rather than in a textual sentence), which would thus, per Table T.6 of *The Bluebook*, allow for abbreviation of words in a case name, such as "Bankruptcy,"

"Development," and "Society." Nevertheless, most practitioners prefer not to abbreviate such words in the table of authorities, and only abbreviate widely known acronyms and the eight words listed in Rule 10.2.1(c), such as "Co." and "Corp.," so that the table, often the first substantive part of a brief reviewed by a reader, has a formal, complete, and professional appearance.

- If you decide to use full case names rather than treating the citations in the table as "stand-alones," as discussed previously, be especially careful when allowing a word processing program to create your table. If on page 6 of your brief, for example, you refer to "*Cooley Agric. Bd. v. Redmond Indem. Co.*, 15 F. Supp. 2d 18 (D.N.J. 1998)," some word processing programs will re-create the citation in your table in exactly that form, requiring you to manually convert the citation to "*Cooley Agriculture Board v. Redmond Indemnity Co.*, 15 F. Supp. 2d 18 (D.N.J. 1998)" for the table of authorities. Whichever method you select, be consistent. Don't show *Adams v. American Communications Co.* and then *Bailey v. Aetna Cas. & Sur. Co.*

- Group your citations together according to the type of authority. For example, first list all the cases together under the heading "Cases," then all of the statutes under the heading "Statutes," then all of the miscellaneous authorities, and so forth. If your brief consists mainly of cases with only a few other authorities, your table will likely have just two categories: "Cases" and "Other Authorities." List primary authorities before you list secondary authorities. Remember that unless court rules require a certain organization, there are no rigid rules regarding preparation of tables of authorities. Consider the reader, and use a presentation that readily communicates information. Some writers follow Rule 1.4 relating to the order of citations in strings as a guideline to the order of citations for a table of authorities.

- Within each grouping, list authorities alphabetically (listing cases alphabetically by plaintiff, such that the *Baker* case appears before the *Franklin* case, which appears before the *Jacobs* case); by ascending number for statutes (such that 15 U.S.C. § 2041 (2006) appears before 15 U.S.C. § 2049 (2006), which appears before 18 U.S.C. § 101 (2006)); and by author's last name (such that an article by Zachary Andrews is listed before one by Amy Zabel).

- Do not include introductory signals (such as *see*) or parenthetical expressions (such as "explaining that . . . ").

- Include subsequent history of a citation (such as *cert. denied* or *aff'd*) inasmuch as it is part of the full citation.

- Omit pinpoint citations in the table of authorities.
- Ensure that each time an authority is mentioned (whether in text or footnotes), the table reflects such. Thus, if your brief includes a reference to a certain case on page 4, and then there is an *id.* reference to the same case on page 5, and a later short form reference to the same case on page 11, the table should reflect that the case is discussed on pages 4, 5, and 11.
- Use *passim* rather than listing each page on which the authority appears if you cite a certain authority on numerous occasions throughout the document.
- Always double-check the table of authorities to ensure that if the table says a certain authority is discussed on pages 10 and 14 of your brief, it is discussed on those pages.

Practice Tip

✓ How does one alphabetize a case name such as *In re Lowrey*? Is it alphabetized under "I" or under "L" as *In re Lowrey*? Unfortunately, there is no good answer to this question. Books of case reports such as *Federal Supplement* alphabetize such cases by the first letter of the party's name, as in *Lowrey, In re;* however, that might be for ease of retrieval when there are numerous cases in the book that begin with the phrase *In re.* A review of briefs filed with the U.S. Supreme Court shows some variation, but most briefs show such cases alphabetized under "I" and presented as follows:

Hunter v. Amoco Products Co.
In re Lowe
In re Peterson
Jackson v. Phillips

Other briefs would place *In re Peterson* with the "P" cases, although they would continue to display it in the table of authorities as *In re Peterson.*

Alphabetize cases in which the United States is a party under "U" as in *United States v. Georgia* and then *United States v. Munoz.*

When in doubt, review briefs filed with the U.S. Supreme Court at the Court's website at http://www.supremecourt.gov to get ideas about setting up tables of authorities.

■ Footnotes

Many legal writers prefer to cite their authorities in footnotes rather than in the narrative portion of the text. Other writers use both techniques in the same document, placing some authorities in the text of the document and others in footnotes. Endnotes (listing all authorities on a separate page at the end of a document) are rarely, if ever, used by legal writers (except in textbooks).

There are two schools of thought on the use of footnotes. Some writers believe that using citations throughout the narrative is distracting and, thus, placing the citations in footnotes facilitates uninterrupted reading of a document. Other writers believe exactly the opposite, reasoning that when readers encounter a footnote either they train themselves to ignore it (in which case, the footnote is of no value) or, indulging a natural curiosity, they jump from the narrative to the footnote to see what it says, thus interrupting the flow of the argument.

Some courts have rules regarding or even prohibiting the citation of authorities in footnotes (realizing that typeface in footnotes is often smaller than that used in the narrative portion of text, thus allowing writers to squeeze more material into a brief and perhaps exceed page limits), and others limit the number of footnotes that may be used. Review these rules, and consult with colleagues in your office to determine if one practice is more favored than another.

If citing authorities in footnotes, consider the following:

- Because footnotes in and of themselves can be distracting, do not distract readers further by appending excessive substantive explanatory parentheticals to cases cited. For example, avoid the following approach: "[1]*Dyer v. Maxwell*, 904 F.2d 118, 130-34 (9th Cir. 1994) (holding that abandonment of a trademark is presumed to have occurred after three years, although the presumption can be overcome by clear and convincing evidence otherwise, such as occurs when the trademark owner has made use of the mark customary in its trade or profession, so long as that use is not merely a token use)." If an issue merits substantive discussion, it likely merits discussion in the body of the work. Moreover, some readers have trained themselves to ignore footnotes, believing information therein is likely to be extraneous to the main argument. Thus, making key arguments in footnotes could well be futile.

- Avoid footnotes that continue or "wrap" from one page to the next. For example, consider a reader who is reviewing page 4 of a brief and encounters a footnote. The reader glances down at the bottom of page 4, begins reading the footnote, and must continue on to pages 5 and 6 to finish reading the footnote. When finished reading the footnote, the reader must return to page 4 and remember where he or she left off. Such a style is terribly distracting for almost all readers. Some will not return to the original page, thus missing significant portions of an analysis.

- If there are several citations within one footnote, the use of *id.* in that footnote will send a reader to the immediately preceding authority within that same footnote. Alternatively, *id.* can be used as a footnote to refer to a preceding separate footnote, as long as there is only one authority cited within that preceding footnote. In brief, *id.* may be used when the preceding citation contains only one source.

- If you are directing a reader to a footnote within a source you cite, indicate as follows: "Harry S. Hunter, Annotation, *Tobacco Litigation*, 78 A.L.R.4th 106, 108 n.14 (1996)." (See Rule 3.2(b).) Note that there is no space between the "n." and the footnote reference. Cite multiple footnotes as follows: "nn.343-47."

- *The Bluebook*'s Rule 1.1 gives instructions and an example on where to place the "call number" (namely, the superscript footnote number, as in ^{2}).

Practice Tip

✓ *The Bluebook* flatly states that practitioners should place their citations in the text of the document (and not use footnotes). B2. This is an oversimplification; many practitioners use footnotes. Follow court rules and your office practice.

Thus, *The Bluebook* position is that whereas those writing law review articles and journals will place citations in footnotes, practitioners place their citations in the narrative text of a document. Nevertheless, many practitioners use footnotes (usually in combination with citations in the text of a document), and they will likely continue to do so, despite *The Bluebook* position.

■ Internal Cross-References (Rule 3.5)

If you wish to send a reader to another part of the brief or document itself, be as specific as possible. Although there is nothing prohibiting you from merely directing the reader, "See Section III, *supra*," it is easier for the reader if you provide the exact page, as follows: "See Section III, *supra* p. 8." This directs the reader to page 8 within your document to review Section III. Note that "p." and "pp." (for "pages") are used only for internal cross-references.

If you are directing a reader to a previous source within your brief, follow the format: "Grant, *supra* p. 2, at 909" (directing the reader to return to page 2 of your brief and then to review page 909 of Charles Grant's book).

If you are directing a reader to a previous footnote within your brief, follow the format: "Grant, *supra* note 23, at 909" (directing the reader to return to footnote number 23 in your brief and then to review page 909 of Charles Grant's book).

Remember that when directing a reader to pages or notes within your brief, *supra* is not followed by a comma (as in "Grant, *supra* note 23, at 909"). When directing a reader to a page within the previously cited authority, *supra* is followed by a comma (as in "Grant, *supra*, at 909").

Practice Tip

✓ Because the addition or deletion of any material from your document will likely cause changes in pagination, insert the internal cross-reference page numbers only when the document is near completion. Use blank lines as you prepare the document, then replace them with actual page numbers just before final typing. Alternatively, you can use a unique combination of letters (perhaps your initials or XOX) instead of blank lines, then use the "find" and "replace" functions on your word processor to replace these initials with the actual page numbers.

■ Final Tasks in Cite-Checking

Before any document that includes citations leaves your office, take the following last steps to ensure the document is accurate:

- Proofread carefully to ensure typists or word processors correctly made the revisions you requested.
- Be alert to inconsistency. If you underscored case names, then book titles and signals should be similarly underscored. Ensure that the document does not switch back and forth between underscoring and italicizing, which can easily occur if more than one author has worked on the document.
- Make sure the final document is printed by one printer because the use of different printers can result in a different appearance among pages.
- Recheck all of the short form signals, such as *id.* and *supra.* If material has either been added to or deleted from a document, these signals could well be incorrect.
- Check the accuracy of each quotation. Quotations must be reproduced scrupulously. If changes are made, make sure they are indicated through the use of ellipses or bracketed information.
- Check to make sure pinpoints are included for all citations.
- Review the table of authorities to ensure that all case names are full and complete (with only commonly known acronyms and words such as "Inc." and "Corp." abbreviated) if this is your office practice and that the references to the pages in the document on which authorities appear are correct. Do not rely exclusively on word processing programs to reproduce the table. Do your own proofreading.

Exercise for **Chapter 9**

Use a separate sheet of paper to create a table of authorities for the following authorities that will be cited in a brief. You might need to supply missing information, make corrections in, and provide additions to the citations. You need not provide a reference to pages on which these authorities would appear in the brief.

Hanover Shoe, Inc. v. United Shoe Machinery Corporation, 392 US 481, 485 (1968)

FDA v. Brown and Williamson Tobacco Corp., 529 US 120 (2000)

Emmert v. Old National Bank, 246 SE2d 236 (W. Va. 1978)

Woodward v. Dain 85 A. 660, 665 (Me. 1913)

Berger v. Nazametz, 157 F.Supp.2d 998 (So. Dist. Ill. 2001)

Downie v. Independent Drivers Ass'n, 934 F. 2d 1168 (Cir. 10 1991)

Bowen v. Georgetown University Hosp., 488 U.S. 204 (1988)

Firestone Tire & Rubber Co. v. Bruch, 489 U.S. 101 (1989)

Manning v. Sheehan, 133 NYS 1006 (N.Y. App. Div. 1931)

Finch v. Wachovia Bank & Trust Co., 577 S.E. 2d 306 (N.C. App. Ct. 2003)

NLRB v. Bell Aerospace Co., 416 U.S. 267 (1974)

In re Sullivan's Will, 12 NW2d 148 (Neb. 1943)

Felix Frankfurter, Some Reflections on the Reading of Statutes, 47 Columbia Law Review 52 (1947)

Edwin R. Keedy, Ignorance and Mistake in the Criminal Law, 22 Harvard L. Rev. 75 (1908)

Restatement Second of Torts § 312 comment b, illustration 2

Restatement Second of Contracts § 131

12 U.S.C. § 1291

12 U.S.C. § 1254

18 USC § 924(a)

18 USC § 924 (d)(1)

47 USC § 223

Ark. Code Ann. § 17-24-512

Ohio Rev. Code Ann. § 2917.21

Md. Code Ann. Commercial Law § 14-203

Fla. Stat. Annotated § 559.77(3)

10 The Final Review

Correct the citations in the following brief and memorandum. The brief is based on an actual brief and was revised (and condensed) to provide a "real-life" example of a court brief. The author wishes to apologize to the authors of the original brief for these revisions and changes. The memorandum is based on a published case, but several errors have been introduced into the memorandum so that it can serve as a tool to teach cite-checking.

You might need to create information such as dates and pinpoints. Follow *Bluebook* rules.

IN THE CIRCUIT COURT OF COOK COUNTY, ILLINOIS
COUNTY DEPARTMENT, LAW DIVISION

Citibank, N.A.,	)	
	)	
Plaintiff,	)	
	)	
vs.	)	No. 2205 L 13222
	)	
McGladrey & Pullen, LLP,	)	Judge Dennis J. Burke
	)	
Defendants.	)	
_____	)	

McGLADREY & PULLEN LLP's MEMORANDUM OF LAW SUPPORTING ITS MOTION FOR SUMMARY JUDGMENT

McGladrey & Pullen LLP respectfully submits the following Memorandum of Law in support of its motion for summary judgment.

I. Background

This case concerns loans that Citibank, N.A. ("Citibank") extended beginning in 2002 to a surgical practice owned by Dr. Mark S. Weinberger, a surgeon who vanished in Europe, along with Citibank's money, in September 2004. When Citibank failed to locate Dr. Weinberger, Citibank sought to recover its losses by suing the accounting firm McGladrey & Pullen LLP ("M & P"), an Iowa limited liability partnership. Citibank has alleged that M & P negligently audited the surgical practice's 2003 balance sheet and that Citibank relied on this audit in making loans to the practice.

II. Legal Standard

Summary judgment is "to be encouraged in the interest of prompt disposition of lawsuits," where appropriate. *Pyne v. Witner*, 543 N.E.2d 1304, 1309-1310 (Ill. 1989). Summary judgment should be granted if the record "show[s] that there is no genuine issue as to any material fact and that the moving party is entitled to a judgment as a matter of law." 735 Ill. Comp. Stat. 5/2-1005(c). A Defendant may support a summary judgment motion either by "(1) affirmatively showing that some element of the cause of action must be resolved in defendant's favor; or (2) by demonstrating that plaintiff cannot produce evidence necessary to support the plaintiff's cause of action". *Medow v. Flavin*, 782 N.E.2d 733, 739 (Ill. Ct. App. 2002).

In a professional negligence case, summary judgment should be granted where the plaintiff cannot make a sufficient factual showing that the defendant's choice of procedures breached the standard of case. See *O'Brien & Associates, P.C. v. Tim Thomson, Inc.*, 653 N.E.2d 956, 961 (Illinois1995).

III. Argument

A. M & P is Entitled to Summary Judgment because Citibank Cannot Prove That M & P's Audit was Wrong.

Although auditors can be liable for shortcomings in audit procedures that result in misrepresentation of a business's financial position, they cannot be liable for shortcomings that do *not* result in the misrepresentation of a business's financial position. *See Danis v. USN Communications Inc.*, 121 F.Supp.2d 1183, 1192 (N.D. Ill. 2000); *Edward J. DeBartolo Corp. v. Coopers & Lybrand*, 928 F. Supp. 557, 563 (W. Dist. Pa. 1996) (hereinafter "*DeBartolo*").

Unless the auditors' opinion is erroneous, shortcomings in their procedures are immaterial and cannot be the basis for malpractice liability. *Danis*, 121 F. Supp 2d at 1192. *DeBartolo*, 928 F. Supp. at 563. Moreover, because Generally Accepted Accounting Principles [hereinafter "GAAP"] are not within the common knowledge of laypersons, the plaintiff bears the burden to provide through expert testimony that the auditor's opinion was erroneous. *Barth v. Reagan*, 564 N.E.2d 1196, 1201 (Ill. 1990).

In *Danis*, the Plaintiffs alleged that an accounting firm negligently overlooked a material overstatement of the company's accounts receivables and that the firm had misrepresented the facts when it certified that it had conducted its audits in accordance with GAAP. No expert testified that the financial statements were materially misstated. The Court therefore ruled that "[i]f the financial statements were not materially misstated as a result of alleged GAAP violations, the accounting firm's assurance of compliance with GAAP was not materially. . .misleading." *Danis*, 121 F. Supp. 2d at 1188-1189.

Here, M & P represented that the practice's "balance sheet. . .presents fairly, in all material respects, the financial position as of December 31, 2003, in conformity with GAAP." Exhibit 3. Citibank has offered no expert testimony that M & P's opinion was wrong or that the 2003 balance sheet was materially misstated. Because Citibank cannot maintain an accounting malpractice case where it cannot prove material accounting errors, the Court should enter summary judgment for M & P.

B.   M & P Is Entitled to Summary Judgment Because the Decision Whether to Use Medical Specialists Was a Protected Judgment Call.

M & P also is entitled to summary judgment for the alternative, independent reason that the decision whether to use medical specialists as part of an audit is a "judgment call" that is immune from liability. "The law distinguishes between mistaken judgments and errors of negligence. A mere error of judgment does not subject [a professional] to liability." *O'Brien*, 653 N.E.2nd at 1001. In *O'Brien*, the Plaintiff alleged that its former lawyers negligently failed to timely join additional parties to a lawsuit. The appeals court affirmed summary judgment for the professionals because "deciding when to join parties is left to the attorney's judgment. A mere error of judgment does not subject [the professional] to liability even if the erroneous judgment leads to an unfavorable outcome." Id.

In *Mishkin v. Peat, Marwick, Mitchell & Company*, 744 F.Supp. 531, 538 (S.D.N.Y. 1990), the plaintiff sued an accounting firm for failing to discover alleged fraud during an audit. The plaintiff alleged that the firm negligently planned, staffed, and supervised the audit, and failed to perform audit procedures that would have detected the fraud. The court entered judgment for the auditors because "staffing, supervision, planning and execution of the audit were judgment calls ... as to which opinions will often differ. *Id.* The court flatly stated "an auditor . . . is not responsible for mere errors of judgment." *Id.* 539.

In the present case, Citibank has alleged that M & P should have used medical professionals to interpret medical records as part of the audit. Ex. 2; Bartko Deposition 90: 1-23 (September 15, 2005). The procedures M & P performed are set forth in various guides relating to auditing health care practices as among the generally accepted procedures for testing health care receivables. Ex. 2 at page 51.

As noted by one court, "the standard is that which is *generally accepted* . . . . It is not sufficient for plaintiff's expert witness to testify that he would have acted differently in the circumstances. (emphasis added) Wilsman v. Sloniewicz, 526 N.E.2d 645, 655 (Ill. App. Ct. 1988).

M & P's decision not to use medical professionals to interpret medical records and instead to perform more commonly used health care audit procedures was a judgment call. Because a professional's judgment call — even if erroneous — cannot breach the standard of care, summary judgment is appropriate. *See O'Brien, supra.*

Conclusion

For the foregoing reasons, M & P respectfully requests that the Court enter an order granting its motion for summary judgment.

Dated: _____

                                        Respectfully submitted,

                                        By: _____

MEMORANDUM

To: Stephen M. Mitchell
From: Allison L. Fisher
Re: Age Discrimination in Employment
Date: December 1

Factual Background

Our client, TechCenter, Inc. ("TechCenter") recently terminated the employment of Ray Harris ("Harris"). Harris has alleged that he was selected for termination because he was nearing his sixtieth birthday and that the termination was thus a violation of the Age Discrimination in Employment Act. Harris was hired two years ago by Gregory Charlton ("Charlton"), a midlevel supervisor at TechCenter, who occasionally called Harris "old-timer." The last performance review that Harris received before his termination rated him as "unsatisfactory" and noted that he was often late to work.

Harris was terminated six months after TechCenter merged with another company. At the time of the merger, TechCenter's President, Jacqueline Allen ("Allen"), announced that she would conduct an analysis to determine if positions within the two companies were duplicative and that redundant or duplicative positions would be eliminated. Allen's analysis concluded that Harris's position was redundant, and Allen formally terminated Harris's employment. At the time Harris was terminated, six other employees were also terminated. Four of those employees were under age 40; two were over age 40.

Analysis

Direct Discrimination

The Age Discrimination in Employment Act ("ADEA") prohibits employers from firing workers who are forty or over on the basis of their age. 29 U.S.C. §623 (2006). To prevail on a claim of age discrimination in firing, a plaintiff may show discrimination either directly or indirectly. *Fass v. Sears, Roebuck and Co.*, 532 F.3d 633 (7th Cir. 2008). In either case, however, the key question is whether the plaintiff has proved intentional discrimination. *Olson v. Northern FS, Inc.*, 387 F.3rd 632, 635 (7th Cir. 2004).

The direct method requires a plaintiff to offer direct or circumstantial evidence that an employer's decision to terminate was motivated by age. *Tubergen v. St. Vincent Hosp. & Health Care Center, Inc.*, 517 F.3d 470, 473

(2nd Cir. 2000). Harris has alleged that the comments by Charlton show that the decision to terminate him was motivated by age. Those comments, however, are only relevant if Charlton was either a decision maker or had singular influence over the decision maker. See *Staub v. Proctor Hospital,* 560 F.3d 647, 651 (3d Cir. 2009). As one court has noted, "generally speaking, comments by a non-decision maker do not suffice as evidence of discriminatory intent." *Lucas v. Chicago Transit Authority,* 367 F. 3d 714, 730 (7th Cir. 2004).

In the present case, the decision maker, Allen, conducted her own analysis into the facts relevant to the decision to terminate various employment positions because they were duplicative. Thus, Charlton's comments are not relevant unless he exercised "singular influence" over Allen and used that influence to cause the adverse employment action. *See Staub.* It seems highly unlikely that Charlton, a midlevel supervisor, would exert this level of influence over TechCenter's president. Thus, Harris cannot prove direct discrimination.

Indirect Discrimination

To establish a prima facie case of age discrimination under the indirect method, a plaintiff must prove all of the following: that he or she is a member of a protected class (namely, that he or she is over forty years of age); that his or her work performance met the company's legitimate expectations; that despite job performance he or she was subject to an adverse employment action; and that the company treated similarly situated employees under forty more favorably. *Fass,* 532 F.3d at 641. In any event, the ultimate burden to provide intentional discrimination always remains with the plaintiff. *Greene v. Potter,* 557 F.3d 765, 769 (8th Cir. 2009), certiorari denied, 550 U. S. 909 (2010).

In the present case, Harris can satisfy the first element of the test (namely, that he is a member of a protected class) because he is over age forty. He will be unable to satisfy the second prong of the test because he will be unable to prove that his work performance met the company's legitimate expectations. First, the company's expectations changed after the merger when the company reasonably decided to eliminate duplicative decisions. Second, Harris's job performance had been unsatisfactory even before the merger. He was not meeting the company's legitimate expectations for its workers.

As to the third prong, it would appear that Harris was terminated both because his position was redundant and because he was an unsatisfactory performer. Thus, Harris cannot prove the third prong of a prima facie case;

Harris was subject to an adverse employment action (namely, termination) *because* of his performance — not despite it.

The final issue is whether TechCenter treated similarly situated employees under forty more favorably. In the present case, of the seven employees who were terminated, four were under forty; three (including Harris) were over forty years. Harris will have an extremely difficult time proving this final prong of a prima facie case because similarly situated employees under the age of forty were not treated more favorably. In fact, more than one-half of the employees terminated were under forty. Harris cannot establish a prima facie case of age discrimination under the indirect method because he cannot prove all four elements of the test. In fact, he can only prove one element: that he is a member of a protected class.

Finally, the U.S. Supreme Court has held that in cases brought under the ADEA, it is not sufficient to show that age was a motivating factor. The plaintiff must prove that, but for his age, the adverse action would not have occurred. *Gross v. FBL Financial Services*, 129 S. Ct. 2343 (2009). Although Harris may be able to show that his age possibly was a factor in the determination to terminate his employment, because his position was duplicative of others after the merger and because he had been rated as an unsatisfactory employee, his age was not a "but for" cause.

Conclusion

Harris will be highly unlikely to show that he was wrongfully terminated in violation of the Age Discrimination in Employment Act because he cannot show that but for his age he would not have been terminated.

Citation Quiz   Chapter 10

Answer the following questions using **Bluebook** *rules.*

1. The following citation is correct: *Jones v. Smith, supra.*

_____

2. The short form *Id.* always appears with an uppercase "I."

_____

3. A section symbol is always followed by a space.

_____

4. The following format is correct: 11th Cir.

_____

5. You must always give parallel citations for all state court cases.

_____

6. Pinpoint citations are needed for both quotations and paraphrases.

_____

7. Quotations of _____ or more words should be indented.

_____

8. Which of the following is correct:
    a.   10 U.S.C. §1244.
    b.   10 USC § 1244.
    c.   10 U.S.C. 1244 (2006).
    d.   10 U.S.C. § 1244 (2006).

_____

9. Which of the following is correct:
    a.   *Id.* at § 102.
    b.   *Id.* § 102.
    c.   Reynolds, *id.*
    d.   *Id.* at p. 455.

_____

10. If a book is authored by two individuals, which of the following is correct:
    a.   John T. Fisher and Mary M. Nelson
    b.   John T. Fisher, et al.
    c.   John T. Fisher & Mary M. Nelson
    d.   Fisher & Nelson

_____

11. Which case name is correct:

   a.   *Gregory Carson v. Jacobson Bros.*

   b.   *Carson v. Jacobson Brothers*

   c.   *Carson v. Jacobson Bros.*

   d.   *Carson v. Jacobson*

---

12. Which citation is correct (assuming there are no local rules):

   a.   *Smith v. Jones*, 901 P.2d 18, 21 (Wash. 1999).

   b.   *Smith v. Jones*, 424 Wash. 2d 401, 405, 901 P.2d 18, 21 (1999).

   c.   *Smith v. Jones*, 424 Wash.2d 401, 405, 901 P.2d 18, 21 (1999).

   d.   *Smith v. Jones*, 901 P.2d 18, 21 (Wash. Supreme Court (1999).

---

13. Which citation is correct:

   a.   *Phillips v. Simmons*, 48 F. Supp. 2d 901, 905-908 (S.D.N.Y. 2005).

   b.   *Phillips v. Simmons*, 48 F. Supp. 2d 901, 905-08 (S.D. N.Y. 2005).

   c.   *Phillips v. Simmons*, 48 F. Supp. 2d 901, 905-08 (S.D.N.Y. 2005).

   d.   *Phillips v. Simmons*, 48 F. Supp. 2d 901, 905-08 (S. Dist. N. Y. 2005).

---

14. Which citation is correct when citing a treatise as a short form:

   a.   Moore, *supra*, at § 101.

   b.   Moore, *Supra*, § 101.

   c.   Moore, *supra* § 101.

   d.   Moore, *supra*, § 101.

---

15. Which citation is correct:

   a.   *United States v. Lawson*, 450 U.S. 19, 21, 201 S. Ct. 90, 93, 89 L. Ed. 2d 430, 435 (2001).

   b.   *United States v. Lawson*, 450 U.S. 19, 21 (2001).

   c.   *U.S. v. Lawson*, 450 U.S. 19, 21 (2001).

   d.   *USA v. Lawson*, 450 U.S. 19, 21 (2001).

Answer Keys

When italics are used in the answer keys, underscoring is also proper.

Exercise for Chapter 2

The following are examples found in the Bluebook. Correct them for use by practitioners.

1. 17 AM. JUR. 2D *Contracts* § 74 (1964).
17 Am. Jur. 2d *Contracts* § 74 (1964).

2. N.M. STAT. ANN. § 4-44-7(G) (1983).
N.M. Stat. Ann. § 4-44-7(G) (1983).

3. FED. R. APP. P. 2.
Fed. R. App. P. 2.

4. RESTATEMENT (THIRD) OF UNFAIR COMPETITION § 3 (1995).
Restatement (Third) of Unfair Competition § 3 (1995).

5. 4 CHARLES ALAN WRIGHT & ARTHUR R. MILLER, FEDERAL PRACTICE AND PROCEDURE § 106 (2d ed. 1987).
4 Charles Alan Wright & Arthur R. Miller, *Federal Practice and Procedure* § 106 (2d ed. 1987).

6. Kim Lane Scheppele, *Foreword: Telling Stories*, 87 Mɪᴄʜ. L. Rᴇᴠ. 2073, 2082 (1989).
   Kim Lane Scheppele, *Foreword: Telling Stories*, 87 Mich. L. Rev. 2073, 2082 (1989).

7. S. Rᴇᴘ. Nᴏ. 84-2, at 7 (1955).
   S. Rep. No. 84-2, at 7 (1955).

Exercise for

Chapter 3

Correct the following citations. You might need to supply or create missing information, such as dates and page numbers. Either make up numbers and dates or use the form "xxx" as in "xxx P.2d xxx." There might be more than one thing wrong with the citation.

Notes:

- Case names and signals may be either underscored or italicized.
- When making up citations, you may use any series of reports. For example, you may use "A." or "A.2d."

Case Names

1. Renee Burnette versus M.L. Parker
   Burnette v. Parker

2. N.P. Hicks, Jr. vs. Andrew J. Koch and Alan R. Ladwig
   Hicks v. Koch

3. State of Ohio versus Manufacturers Engineering Coalition Association, a state court case (Assume the citation appears as a "stand-alone" citation.)
   State v. Mfrs. Eng'g Coal. Ass'n

4. State of Ohio versus Manufacturers Engineering Coalition Association, a state court case (Assume the citation appears as part of a textual sentence.)
   State v. Manufacturers Engineering Coalition Ass'n

5. Southern Casualty and Indemnity Company versus USA (Cite first assuming the citation appears in a textual sentence and then cite as a stand-alone citation.)
    Southern Casualty & Indemnity Co. v. United States (in textual sentence)
    S. Cas. & Indem. Co. v. United States (in stand-alone citation)

6. James & Susan Lovell versus the Federal Communications Commission
    Lovell v. FCC (Per Rule 6.1(b), *Lovell v. Federal Communications Commission* is also correct, but *Lovell v. FCC* is preferred.)

7. Judith D. Harris vs. O'Hara, et al.
    Harris v. O'Hara

State Court Cases

8. McBride v. Murphy, 304 Kansas Reports 123 (2006) (Assume the citation appears in a brief submitted to a court requiring parallel citations.)
    McBride v. Murphy, 304 Kan. 123, xxx P.2d xxx (2006)

9. Danielson v. Franklin Corporation, 86 New York Reports, Second Series, at page 111, 640 New York Supplement, Second Series 766, 690 North Eastern Reporter, Second Series, 211 (2004) (Cite first assuming the citation appears in a brief submitted to a court requiring parallel citations and then cite assuming the citation appears in a letter to a client.)
    Danielson v. Franklin Corp., 86 N.Y.2d 111, 690 N.E.2d 211, 640 N.Y.S.2d 766 (2004) [Note: An example is found on page 11 of *The Bluebook*]
    Danielson v. Franklin Corp., 690 N.E.2d 211 (N.Y. 2004)

10. Smith v. Michaelson, a 2009 case from the Connecticut Appellate Court (Cite first assuming the citation appears in a brief submitted to a court requiring parallel citations and then cite assuming the citation appears in a letter to a client.)
    Smith v. Michaelson, xxx Conn. App. xxx, xxx A.2d xxx (2009)
    Smith v. Michaelson, xxx A.2d xxx (Conn. App. Ct. 2009)

11. Ruiz v. Jacobsen Brothers, a 2007 case from the Iowa Supreme Court.
    Ruiz v. Jacobsen Bros., xxx N.W.2d xxx (Iowa 2007)

12. Parker v. Tech Inc., a 2006 case from the Iowa Court of Appeals.
    Parker v. Tech Inc., xxx N.W.2d xxx (Iowa Ct. App. 2006)

13. Simmons & Simmons Co. v. Gregson, a 2009 case from the Arizona Court of Appeals (Assume court rules require parallel citations.)

> *Simmons & Simmons Co. v. Gregson,* xxx Ariz. xxx, xxx P.3d xxx (Ct. App. 2009).
>
> [Note: Because the set *Arizona Reports* publishes cases from both the Arizona Supreme Court and the Arizona Court of Appeals, the parenthetical must include the information that the case was decided by the Arizona Court of Appeals but need not repeat "Ariz." A reference in a parenthetical to "Ariz." would imply that the case was decided by the Arizona Supreme Court.]

14. Give the public domain citation (with pinpoints) for the 2004 Oklahoma case *Mansfield versus Harrison.*

> *Mansfield v. Harrison,* 2004 OK xx, ¶ x, xxx P.2d xxx, xxx.

Federal Cases and Subsequent History

15. Knudson v. Micro Strategy Inc., 540 United States Reports 544, 213 Lawyers Edition, Second Series 967, 203 Supreme Court Reporter 118 (2005).

> *Knudson v. Micro Strategy Inc.,* 540 U.S. 544 (2005)

16. Mitchell v. ABC Co., a 2009 Third Circuit case located in volume 311 of the Federal Reporter, Third Series, at page 802 (Assume certiorari was denied for this case by the U.S. Supreme Court in 2010.)

> *Mitchell v. ABC Co.,* 311 F.3d 802 (3d Cir. 2009), *cert. denied,* xxx U.S. xxx (2010).

17. Pritchett v. Bailey, 799 Federal Reporter, Second Series, page 100, decided by the Ninth Circuit Court of Appeals in 2008 and reversed by the U.S. Supreme Court in that same year.

> *Pritchett v. Bailey,* 799 F.2d 100 (9th Cir.), *rev'd,* xxx U.S. xxx (2008).
>
> [Note: Per Rule 10.5(d), when the date in the two parentheticals will be the same, include the date only in the second parenthetical.]

18. Alvarez v. Nickles, a 2008 case from the U.S. District Court for the Central District of California.

> *Alvarez v. Nickles,* xxx F. Supp. 2d xxx (C.D. Cal. 2008)

19. Harvey v. Phillips, a 2001 case from the U.S. District Court for the District of Delaware and affirmed in 2002 by the Third Circuit Court of Appeals.

> *Harvey v. Phillips,* xxx F. Supp. 2d xxx (D. Del. 2001), *aff'd,* xxx F.3d xxx (3d Cir. 2002)

Spacing

20. 101 Federal Reporter, Third Series 901
      101 F.3d 901

21. 11 American Law Reports, Sixth Series 489
      11 A.L.R.6th 489

22. 14 Southern Reporter, Third Series 399
      14 So. 3d 399

23. 689 Pacific Reporter, Second Series 320
      689 P.2d 320

24. 40 Federal Supplement, Second Series 430
      40 F. Supp. 2d 430

25. 42 Boston University Law Review 607
      42 B.U. L. Rev. 607

26. 12 New York University Environmental Law Journal 977
      12 N.Y.U. Envtl. L.J. 977

27. 344 New York Supplement, Second Series 175
      344 N.Y.S.2d 175

28. U.S. District Court for the Southern District of Ohio
      S.D. Ohio

29. U.S. District Court for the District of New Jersey
      D.N.J.

Exercise for **Chapter 4**

Correct the following citations. You might need to supply missing information.

1. Tenth Amendment to the U.S. Constitution.
      U.S. Const. amend. X.

2. Article 1, Section 8, clause three of the U.S. Constitution.
      U.S. Const. art. 1, § 8, cl. 3.

3. Article 10 of the Nevada Constitution.
> Nev. Const. art. 10.

4. House of Representatives bill number 4213, 111th Congress.
> Title of Proposed Legislation, H.R. 4213, 111th Cong. (20xx) or Title
> of Proposed Legislation, H.R. 4213, 111th Cong. § x (20xx).
> [Note: The name of the bill is included, if relevant.]

5. Section 3 of Senate bill number 2711, 107th Congress.
> Title of Proposed Legislation, S. 2711, 107th Cong. § 3 (20xx).
> [Note: The name of the bill is included, if relevant.]

6. "The End to Discriminatory State Taxes for Automobile Renters Act of
2009." Hearing on H.R. 4175 before the House Committee on the Judiciary, statement of Representative John Conyers, Jr. (110th Congress)
> *The End to Discriminatory State Taxes for Automobile Renters Act*
> *of 2009: Hearing on H.R. 4175 Before the S. Comm. on the Judi-*
> *ciary*, 110th Cong. xx (20xx) (statement of Rep. John Conyers, Jr.).

7. Statement of Senator Christopher J. Dodd, volume 155, pages 113-118
of the Congressional Record.
> 155 Cong. Rec. 113-18 (year) (statement of Sen. Christopher J.
> Dodd).

8. Title 18, section 4422 of the United States Code.
> 18 U.S.C. § 4422 (2006).

9. Title 42, section 1044 of the United States Code Annotated.
> 42 U.S.C.A. § 1044 (West year).

10. Title 7, sections 1051 through 1059 of the United States Code Service.
Assume this statute is located only in the pocket part of the set.
> 7 U.S.C.S. §§ 1051-1059 (LexisNexis Supp. year).

11. New York General Construction Law, section 1420.
> N.Y. Gen. Constr. Law § 1420 (Publisher year).

12. Section 10-42-109 of the Montana Code Annotated.
> Mont. Code Ann. § 10-42-109 (year).

13. Texas Government Code Annotated section 2422.
> Tex. Gov't Code Ann. § 2422 (West year).

14. Arizona Revised Statutes Annotated section 10-325.
> Ariz. Rev. Stat. Ann. § 10-325 (year).

15. Federal Rule of Civil Procedure 26(a).
Fed. R. Civ. P. 26(a).

16. Uniform Securities Act section 302.
Unif. Sec. Act § 302, x U.L.A. xx (year).

17. Senate Report Number 230 from the 108th Congress, page 34.
S. Rep. No. 108-230, at 34 (year).

Exercise for **Chapter 5**

Correct the following citations. You might need to supply missing information.

1. Volume 64 of Am. Jur. 2d, section 104, discussing "trusts."
64 Am. Jur. 2d *Trusts* § 104 (year).

2. Volume 13 of Cal. Jur. 3d, section 11, discussing "battery."
13 Cal. Jur. 3d *Battery* § 11 (year).

3. Page 714 of the current edition of *Black's Law Dictionary*, defining the word "inchoate."
Black's Law Dictionary 714 (9th ed. 2009).

4. Volume 4 of the set of books titled "Wills, Trusts, and Estate Planning" by Ronald Cresswell, Sarah Patel Pacheco, and Patrick Pacheco, second edition, section 3:44.
4 Ronald Cresswell, Sarah Patel Pacheco & Patrick Pacheco, *Wills, Trusts, and Estate Planning* § 3:44 (2d ed. year) or
4 Ronald Cresswell et al., *Wills, Trusts, and Estate Planning* § 3:44 (2d ed. year).

5. Section 201 of the Restatement of Agency, Third.
Restatement (Third) of Agency § 201 (year).

6. Sections 101 through 104 of the Restatement of the Law, Second, Conflict of Laws, comment b.
Restatement (Second) Conflict of Laws §§ 101-104 cmt. b (year).

7. Volume 2 of the fourth edition of "Insurance Law Handbook," written by Hillary R. Reynolds, paragraph 104.

2 Hillary R. Reynolds, *Insurance Law Handbook* ¶ 104 (4th ed. year).

8. A law review article authored by Sam Kamin in 2005, located in volume 46 and beginning at page 83 of the Boston College Law Review and entitled "The Private Is Public: The Relevance of Private Actors in Defining the Fourth Amendment."

Sam Kamin, *The Private Is Public: The Relevance of Private Actors in Defining the Fourth Amendment*, 46 B.C. L. Rev. 83 (2005).

9. Volume 104 of C.J.S., sections 104 through 110, discussing "Trespass."

104 C.J.S. *Trespass* §§ 104-110 (year).

10. A 2010 law review article authored by Stephen L. Logonsky, Jr., entitled "Restructuring Immigration Adjudication" and located at volume 59, page 1635, of the Duke Law Journal.

Stephen L. Logonsky, Jr., *Restructuring Immigration Adjudication*, 59 Duke L.J. 1635 (2010).

11. An annotation authored by Daniel H. White, entitled "Allowance of Attorneys' Fees Under the Clayton Act," published in volume 21 of A.L.R. Federal, beginning at page 750.

Daniel H. White, Annotation, *Allowance of Attorneys' Fees Under the Clayton Act*, 21 A.L.R. Fed. 750 (year).

12. An annotation authored by Charles W. Benton at volume 43, page 149 of A.L.R. (5th) and entitled "Coverage Provisions in Automobile Liability Policies."

Charles W. Benton, Annotation, *Coverage Provisions in Automobile Liability Policies*, 43 A.L.R.5th 149 (year).

Exercise for Chapter 6

Correct each citation. You might need to supply or create missing information. Assume citations are "stand-alone" citations. Per B7.1.1, citations to court documents may optionally be enclosed in parentheses.

1. "National Organic Program," volume 75 of the Federal Register, page 14500 (March 26, 2010), to be codified at 7 CFR part 205.
   National Organic Program, 75 Fed. Reg. 14,500 (Mar. 26, 2010) (to be codified at 7 C.F.R. pt. 205).

2. Title 37 of the Code of Federal Regulations, Section 263.3 (2009).
   37 C.F.R. § 263.3 (2009).

3. Section 4.34 of title 15 of the Code of Federal Regulations.
   15 C.F.R. § 4.34 (year).

4. Executive Order 13,505 (assume the material is available in C.F.R.).
   Exec. Order No. 13,505, 3 C.F.R. xxx (year).

5. Presidential Proclamation Number 8347 (assume the material is not available in C.F.R.).
   Proclamation No. 8347 or
   Proclamation No, 8347, xx Fed. Reg. xx,xxx (exact date).

6. The registered trademark (Reg. No. 3,567,779) "Silent Running."
   SILENT RUNNING, Registration No. 3,567,779.

7. The case *Black v. United States*, published at 550 U.S. 405 (but also available at the U.S. Supreme Court website).
   Black v. United States, 550 U.S. 405 (year), *available at* www.supremecourt.gov.
   [Note: Website address may be "made up."]

8. An October 24, 2009, article entitled "Coverage Under the Fair Labor Standards Act," written by Camille T. Taylor and available only at the Department of Labor website, http://www.dol.gov/whd/regs/compliance/whdfs14.htm.
   Camille T. Taylor, *Coverage Under the Fair Labor Standards Act*, Dep't of Lab. (Oct. 24, 2009), http://www.dol.gov/whd/regs/compliance/whdfs14.htm
   [Note: *Bluebook* Rule 18.2.2 requires a main page "title," which should be abbreviated per Table T.13. In this case, the article is located at the website of the Department of Labor.]

9. A Motion to Dismiss by all three defendants in a case (page 17).
   Defs.' Mot. to Dismiss 17 or Defs.' Mot. Dismiss 17.
   [Note: Per the example on the inside back cover of *The Bluebook*, the second form is preferable.]

10. Paragraphs 24 through 29 of Defendant's Counterclaim.
    Def.'s Countercl. ¶¶ 24-29.

11. Page 230 of defendant Franklin S. Bailey's deposition, taken September 15, 2009.
    Bailey Dep. 230:xx-xx, Sept. 15, 2009.

12. Exhibit B to Plaintiff's Complaint.
    Pl.'s Compl. Ex. B.

13. *In re Willis Roof Consulting, Inc.*, located in volume 4 of the Labor Law Reporter, paragraph 8410. This case was decided by the U.S. District Court for the Eastern District of Wisconsin in 2004.
    In re Willis Roof Consulting, Inc., 4 Lab. L. Rep. (CCH) ¶ 8410 (E.D. Wis. 2004).
    [Note: An exact date must be given if the case appears in a looseleaf service rather than in a hardbound volume.]

14. The unpublished case Reynolds v. Animal Care Clinics, Inc. decided in November 2009 by the U.S. District Court for the Middle District of Pennsylvania, Westlaw 34644.
    Reynolds v. Animal Care Clinics, Inc., No. xx-xxx, 2009 WL 34644 (M.D. Pa. Nov. xx, 2009).
    [Note: A pincite may be included before the parenthetical.]

15. The unpublished case Jacobson v. ADF, Inc., decided by the Ninth Circuit in January 2010, Lexis 22567.
    Jacobson v. ADF, Inc., No. xx-xxxx, 2010 U.S. App. LEXIS 22567 (9th Cir. Jan. xx, 2010).
    [Note: A pincite may be included before the parenthetical.]

Exercise for **Chapter 7**

Correct the following statements and citations. There might be more than one thing wrong with each citation, and you might need to create missing information. Unless otherwise directed, assume that state court cases are being cited in internal office memoranda.

1. In United States of America versus Bailey, 444 U.S. 394, 409-410, the Court noted that "there is no federal statute defining ... the elements of the duress defense."

   > In *United States v. Bailey*, 444 U.S. 394, 409-10 (year), the Court noted that "there is no federal statute defining . . . the elements of the duress defense."

2. Show that the case in question 1 was decided by a five to four decision and that the quotation appeared on the first page of the case.

   > *United States v. Bailey*, 444 U.S. 394, 394 (year) (5-4 decision).

3. "A district court must retain the absolute control and power to insist upon some specificity in pleading before allowing a potentially massive factual controversy to proceed." *Bell Atlantic Corp. v. Twombly*, 550 U.S. 544, 546-548 (2007).

   a. Fix any errors in the citation.

   > *Bell Atl. Corp. v. Twombly*, 550 U.S. 544, 546-48 (2007).

   b. Show that the foregoing quotation appears on page 558.

   > *Bell Atl. Corp. v. Twombly*, 550 U.S. 544, 558 (2007).

   c. Omit the phrase "absolute control and" from the quotation.

   > "A district court must retain the . . . power to insist upon some specificity in pleading before allowing a potentially massive factual controversy to proceed."

   d. Show how to emphasize the word "absolute" in the foregoing quotation and eliminate the words "before allowing a potentially massive factual controversy to proceed."

   > "A district court must retain the *absolute* control and power to insist upon some specificity in pleading . . . ." *Bell Atl. Corp. v. Twombly*, 550 U.S. 544, 558 (2007) (emphasis added).

   e. Indicate that the quotation is from a dissent by Justice Stevens.

   > *Bell Atl. Corp. v. Twombly*, 550 U.S. 544, 558 (2007) (Stevens, J., dissenting).

   f. Change the first three words ("A district court") to "District courts."

   > "[D]istrict court[s] must retain the absolute power . . . ."

4. "A grant of summary judgment is always reviewed de novo." Reliance Insurance Company v. McGrath, 671 Federal Supplement, Second Series at page 669, decided by the Northern District of California in 1997.

In a single citation, show all of the following:

a. Show that the case was decided by a 3-0 decision.

b. Show that the case was affirmed by the Ninth Circuit the next year in volume 110 of the Federal Reporter, Third Series, at page 102.

c. Show that you emphasized the word "always."

> "A grant of summary judgment is *always* reviewed de novo." *Reliance Ins. Co. v. McGrath*, 671 F. Supp. 2d 669, xxx (N.D. Cal. 1997) (3-0 decision), (emphasis added), *aff'd*, 110 F.3d 102 (9th Cir. 1998).

5. Fix any errors in the following string citation.

Equitable estoppel may apply where there has been an admission, statement, or act that has been justifiably relied upon to the detriment of another party. *Keller v. Prince George's County*, 827 F.2d 952, 964 (4th Cir. 1987), which cited Patsy v. Board of Regents, 457 U.S. 496, 515 (1982). Avery v. County of Burke, 660 F.2d 111, 114,115 (4th Cir. 1981). *Theilmann v. Rutland Hospital, Inc.*, 825 F.2d 853, 855 (2d Cir. 1987); *Allen v. Bullis*, 124 P.3rd 190, 198 (Wash. Ct. App. 2001). *Estate of Lyons v. Sorenson*, 83 Wash.2d 105,108, 515 P.2d 1293 (1973); *Young v. Estate of Snell*, 948 P.2d 1291 (Wash. 1997); *People v. Monterroso* 101 P.3d 956 (Cal. 2004).

> Equitable estoppel may apply where there has been an admission, statement, or act that has been justifiably relied upon to the detriment of another party. *Keller v. Prince George's Cnty.*, 827 F.2d 952, 964 (4th Cir. 1987) (citing *Patsy v. Bd. of Regents*, 457 U.S. 496, 515 (1982)); *Theilmann v. Rutland Hosp., Inc.*, 825 F.2d 111, 114-15 (2d Cir. 1987); *Avery v. Cnty. of Burke*, 660 F.2d 111, 114-15 (4th Cir. 1981); *People v. Monterroso*, 101 P.3d 956, xxx (Cal. 2004); *Young v. Estate of Snell*, 948 P.2d 1291, xxxx (Wash. 1997); *Estate of Lyons v. Sorenson*, 515 P.2d 1293, xxxx (Wash. 1973); *Allen v. Bullis*, 124 P.3d 190, 198 (Wash. Ct. App. 2001).

Exercise for **Chapter 8**

A. Correct the following. Assume that each number to the left of a question refers to a page within a brief being submitted to a court in your state and that there are no intervening citations between questions. If alternative forms of citation are acceptable, give all. Assume the citations are "stand-alone" citations.

1. *Scheuer v. Rhodes*, 416 United States Reports 232, 236, a 1974 case.

   Scheuer v. Rhodes, 416 U.S. 232, 236 (1974).

2. Refer to page 340 of the *Scheuer* case.

   Id. at 340.

3. A 2009 law review article by Richard A. Nagareda titled "Class Certi-fication in the Age of Aggregate Proof," and published at volume 84, page 97 of the New York University Law Review, with a pincite of page 131.

   Richard A. Nagareda, *Class Certification in the Age of Aggregate Proof*, 84 N.Y.U. L. Rev. 97, 131 (2009).

4. Refer to page 139 of the law review article.

   Id. at 139.

5. Volume 4 of the treatise *The Business Judgment Rule*, third edition, 2008, section 12:20, written by Alexander F. Drummond.

   4 Alexander F. Drummond, *The Business Judgment Rule* § 12:20 (3d ed. 2008).

6. Refer to section 12:45 of the previous treatise.

   Id. § 12:45.

7. Refer to page 150 of the law review article.

   Nagareda, *supra*, at 150.

8. Refer to page 342 of the *Scheuer* case.

   Scheuer, 416 U.S. at 342 or

   416 U.S. at 342.

9. Refer to section 12:49 of the treatise by Alexander F. Drummond.

   Drummond, *supra*, § 12:49.

B. Correct the following and describe the meaning of any signal used.

1. See also Asahi Glass Co. v. Pentech Pharmaceuticals, Inc., 289 Federal Supplement, Second Series 986, 995 (Northern District Illinois).

   See also Asahi Glass Co. v. Pentech Pharm., Inc., 289 F. Supp. 2d 986, 995 (N.D. Ill. year).

   (The signal *see also* means that the *Asahi* case constitutes an additional source that supports the proposition. Other authorities that state or directly support the proposition have already been cited.)

2. Cf. DM Research, Inc. v. College of American Pathologists, 170 F. 3rd 53, 56, (First Circuit 1999).

Cf. DM Research, Inc. v. Coll. of Am. Pathologists, 170 F.3d 53, 56
(1st Cir. 1999).

(The signal *cf.* means that the *DM Research* case supports a proposition different from the main proposition but is sufficiently
analogous to lend support. Literally, *cf.* means "compare.")

3. For additional discussion of this topic, see 1 Wayne R. LaFave, Substantive Criminal Law § 5.1 (second edition 2003).

For additional discussion of this topic, see 1 Wayne R. LaFave,
Substantive Criminal Law § 5.1 (2d ed. 2003).

(In this example, the word "see" is being used as an ordinary verb
rather than a signal, and thus, it is neither underscored nor italicized.)

C. Correct the following statements made in a brief submitted to a court.

The plaintiff in this case has vigorously argued that she has been
deprived of her right under the seventh amendment to the USA constitution to a fair trial. The facts, however, show that the plaintiff and defendant
entered into a valid agreement to arbitrate any claims they may have had
against each other. In fact, plaintiff's prior motion for summary judgment
(paragraphs 34 through 40) acknowledges the existence of the arbitration
agreement. Moreover, as noted by justice Sandra Day O'Connor, "[a]n
agreement to arbitrate is as binding as any other agreement." Morrissette
v. United States, 447 U.S. 16, 18 (2007), which was quoted in volume 8 of
the treatise titled "Newburg on Class Actions," and authored by William
B. Rubenstein, et al., Section 24:115. The present case is quite unlike
Morrissette, in which the court found the plaintiff had never agreed to
arbitration.

> The Plaintiff in this case has vigorously argued that she has been
> deprived of her right under the Seventh Amendment to the United
> States Constitution to a fair trial. The facts, however, show that the
> Plaintiff and Defendant entered into a valid agreement to arbitrate
> any claims they may have had against each other. In fact, Plaintiff's
> prior Motion for Summary Judgment acknowledges the existence
> of the arbitration agreement. Pl.'s Mot. Summ. J. ¶¶ 34-40. More-
> over, as noted by Justice Sandra Day O'Connor, "[a]n agreement
> to arbitrate is as binding as any other agreement." *Morrissette v.
> United States,* 447 U.S. 16, 18 (2007), *quoted in* 8 William B.
> Rubenstein et al., *Newberg on Class Actions* § 24:115 (year). The
> present case is quite unlike *Morrissette*, in which the Court
> found the plaintiff had never agreed to arbitration. 447 U.S. at xx.

Exercise for Chapter 9

Use a separate sheet of paper to create a table of authorities for the following authorities that will be cited in a brief. You might need to supply missing information, make corrections in, and provide additions to the citations. You need not provide a reference to pages on which these authorities would appear in the brief.

Notes:

- Any words shown here in italics may be underscored.
- Words in case names that appear in Table T.6 may be abbreviated.
- When a publisher's name is included in a parenthetical for a statute citation, another publisher may be acceptable.
- The order in "Other Authorities" is pursuant to *Bluebook* Rule 1.4(i).
- The placement of the case *In re Sullivan's Will* may vary according to preference.

Cases

Berger v. Nazametz, 157 F. Supp. 2d 998 (S.D. Ill. 2001)
Bowen v. Georgetown University Hospital, 488 U.S. 204 (1988)
Downie v. Independent Drivers Ass'n, 934 F.2d 1168 (10th Cir. 1991)
Emmert v. Old National Bank, 246 S.E.2d 236 (W. Va. 1978)
FDA v. Brown & Williamson Tobacco Corp., 529 U.S. 120 (2000)
Finch v. Wachovia Bank & Trust Co., 577 S.E.2d 306 (N.C. Ct. App. 2003)
Firestone Tire & Rubber Co. v. Bruch, 489 U.S. 101 (1989)
Hanover Shoe, Inc. v. United Shoe Machinery Corp., 392 U.S. 481 (1968)
In re Sullivan's Will, 12 N.W.2d 148 (Neb. 1943)
Manning v. Sheehan, 133 N.Y.S. 1006 (App. Div. 1931)
NLRB v. Bell Aerospace Co., 416 U.S. 267 (1974)
Woodward v. Dain, 85 A. 660 (Me. 1913)

Statutes

12 U.S.C. § 1254 (2006)
12 U.S.C. § 1291 (2006)
18 U.S.C. § 924(a) (2006)
18 U.S.C. § 924(d)(1) (2006)
47 U.S.C. § 223 (2006)
Ark. Code Ann. § 17-24-512 (year)
Fla. Stat. Ann. § 559.77(3) (West year)
Md. Code Ann., Com. Law § 14-203 (LexisNexis year)
Ohio Rev. Code Ann. § 2917.21 (LexisNexis year)

Other Authorities

Restatement (Second) of Contracts § 131 (year)
Restatement (Second) of Torts § 312 cmt. b, illus. 2 (year)
Felix Frankfurter, *Some Reflections on the Reading of Statutes*, 47 Colum.
L. Rev. 52 (1947)
Edwin R. Keedy, *Ignorance and Mistake in the Criminal Law*, 22 Harv. L. Rev.
75 (1908)

Chapter Ten: The Final Review

Correct the citations in the following brief and memorandum. The brief
is based on an actual brief and was revised (and condensed) to provide a
"real-life" example of a court brief. The author wishes to apologize to
the authors of the original brief for these revisions and changes. The
memorandum is based on a published case, but several errors have been
introduced into the memorandum so that it can serve as a tool to teach
cite-checking.

You might need to create information such as dates and pinpoints.
Follow *Bluebook* rules.

Note the following as you make your corrections:

- Underscoring rather than italicizing is acceptable (as long as it is done consistently throughout a document).
- Pinpoint citations have been added because they are critical and allow the reader to readily locate information.
- Note that periods and commas must appear inside quotation marks.
- Citations to court and litigation documents can optionally be placed in parentheses.

IN THE CIRCUIT COURT OF COOK COUNTY, ILLINOIS
COUNTY DEPARTMENT, LAW DIVISION

Citibank, N.A.,	)	
	)	
Plaintiff,	)	
	)	
vs.	)	No. 2205 L 13222
	)	
McGladrey & Pullen, LLP,	)	Judge Dennis J. Burke
	)	
Defendants.	)	
	)	

McGLADREY & PULLEN LLP'S MEMORANDUM OF LAW
SUPPORTING ITS MOTION FOR SUMMARY JUDGMENT

McGladrey & Pullen LLP respectfully submits the following Memorandum of Law in support of its Motion for Summary Judgment.

I. Background

This case concerns loans that Citibank, N.A. ("Citibank") extended beginning in 2002 to a surgical practice owned by Dr. Mark S. Weinberger, a surgeon who vanished in Europe, along with Citibank's money, in September 2004. When Citibank failed to locate Dr. Weinberger, Citibank sought to recover its losses by suing the accounting firm McGladrey & Pullen LLP ("M & P"), an Iowa limited liability partnership. Citibank has alleged that M & P negligently audited the surgical practice's 2003 balance sheet and that Citibank relied on this audit in making loans to the practice.

II. Legal Standard

Summary judgment is "to be encouraged in the interest of prompt disposition of lawsuits," where appropriate. *Pyne v. Witner*, 543 N.E.2d 1304, 1309-10 (Ill. 1989). Summary judgment should be granted if the record "show[s] that there is no genuine issue as to any material fact and that the moving party is entitled to a judgment as a matter of law." 735 Ill. Comp. Stat. 5/2-1005(c) (2009). A defendant may support a summary judgment motion either by "(1) affirmatively showing that some element of the cause of action must be resolved in defendant's favor; or (2) by demonstrating that plaintiff cannot produce evidence necessary to support the plaintiff's cause of action." *Medow v. Flavin*, 782 N.E.2d 733, 739 (Ill. App. Ct. 2002).

In a professional negligence case, summary judgment should be granted where the plaintiff cannot make a sufficient factual showing that the defendant's choice of procedures breached the standard of case. *See O'Brien & Assocs., P.C. v. Tim Thomson, Inc.*, 653 N.E.2d 956, 961 (Ill. 1995).

III. Argument

A. *M & P Is Entitled to Summary Judgment Because Citibank Cannot Prove That M & P's Audit Was Wrong.*

Although auditors can be liable for shortcomings in audit procedures that result in misrepresentation of a business's financial position, they cannot be liable for shortcomings that do *not* result in the misrepresentation of a business's financial position. *See Danis v. USN Commc'ns Inc.*, 121 F. Supp. 2d 1183, 1192 (N.D. Ill. 2000); *Edward J. DeBartolo Corp. v. Coopers & Lybrand*, 928 F. Supp. 557, 563 (W.D. Pa. 1996) [hereinafter *DeBartolo*]. Unless the auditors' opinion is erroneous, shortcomings in their procedures are immaterial and cannot be the basis for malpractice liability. *Danis*, 121 F. Supp. 2d at 1192; *DeBartolo*, 928 F. Supp. at 563. Moreover, because Generally Accepted Accounting Principles [hereinafter "GAAP"] are not within the common knowledge of laypersons, the plaintiff bears the burden to provide through expert testimony that the auditor's opinion was erroneous. *Barth v. Reagan*, 564 N.E.2d 1196, 1201 (Ill. 1990).

In *Danis*, the plaintiffs alleged that an accounting firm negligently overlooked a material overstatement of the company's accounts receivables and that the firm had misrepresented the facts when it certified that it had conducted its audits in accordance with GAAP. No expert testified that the financial statements were materially misstated. The court therefore ruled that "[i]f the financial statements were not materially misstated as a result of alleged GAAP violations, the accounting firm's assurance of compliance with GAAP was not materially... misleading." *Danis*, 121 F. Supp. 2d at 1188-89.

Here, M & P represented that the practice's "balance sheet... presents fairly, in all material respects, the financial position as of December 31, 2003, in conformity with GAAP." Ex. 3. Citibank has offered no expert testimony that M & P's opinion was wrong or that the 2003 balance sheet was materially misstated. Because Citibank cannot maintain an accounting malpractice case where it cannot prove material accounting errors, the Court should enter summary judgment for M & P.

B.   M & P Is Entitled to Summary Judgment Because the Decision Whether to Use Medical Specialists Was a Protected Judgment Call.

M & P also is entitled to summary judgment for the alternative, independent reason that the decision whether to use medical specialists as part of an audit is a "judgment call" that is immune from liability. "The law distinguishes between mistaken judgments and errors of negligence. A mere error of judgment does not subject [a professional] to liability." *O'Brien*, 653 N.E.2d at 1001. In *O'Brien*, the plaintiff alleged that its former lawyers negligently failed to timely join additional parties to a lawsuit. The appeals court affirmed summary judgment for the professionals because "deciding when to join parties is left to the attorney's judgment. A mere error of judgment does not subject [the professional] to liability even if the erroneous judgment leads to an unfavorable outcome." *Id.*

In *Mishkin v. Peat, Marwick, Mitchell & Co.*, 744 F. Supp. 531, 538 (S.D.N.Y. 1990), the plaintiff sued an accounting firm for failing to discover alleged fraud during an audit. The plaintiff alleged that the firm negligently planned, staffed, and supervised the audit, and failed to perform audit procedures that would have detected the fraud. The court entered judgment for the auditors because "staffing, supervision, planning and execution of the audit were judgment calls... as to which opinions will often differ." *Id.* The court flatly stated, "an auditor... is not responsible for mere errors of judgment." *Id.* at 539.

In the present case, Citibank has alleged that M & P should have used medical professionals to interpret medical records as part of the audit. Ex. 2; Bartko Dep. 90:1-23, Sept. 15, 2005. The procedures M & P performed are set forth in various guides relating to auditing health care practices as among the generally accepted procedures for testing health care receivables. Ex. 2, at 51.

As noted by one court, "the standard is that which is *generally accepted....* [I]t is not sufficient for plaintiff's expert witness to testify that he would have acted differently in the circumstances." *Wilsman v. Sloniewicz*, 526 N.E.2d 645, 655 (Ill. App. Ct. 1988) (emphasis added).

M & P's decision not to use medical professionals to interpret medical records and instead to perform more commonly used health care audit procedures was a judgment call. Because a professional's judgment call — even if erroneous — cannot breach the standard of care, summary judgment is appropriate. *See O'Brien*, 653 N.E.2d at 1003.

Conclusion

For the foregoing reasons, M & P respectfully requests that the Court enter an order granting its Motion for Summary Judgment.

Dated: _____

Respectfully submitted,

By: _____

MEMORANDUM

To: Stephen M. Mitchell
From: Allison L. Fisher
Re: Age Discrimination in Employment
Date: December 1

Factual Background

Our client, TechCenter, Inc. ("TechCenter") recently terminated the employment of Ray Harris ("Harris"). Harris has alleged that he was selected for termination because he was nearing his sixtieth birthday and that the termination was thus a violation of the Age Discrimination in Employment Act. Harris was hired two years ago by Gregory Charlton ("Charlton"), a midlevel supervisor at TechCenter, who occasionally called Harris "old-timer." The last performance review that Harris received before his termination rated him as "unsatisfactory" and noted that he was often late to work.

Harris was terminated six months after TechCenter merged with another company. At the time of the merger, TechCenter's President, Jacqueline Allen ("Allen"), announced that she would conduct an analysis to determine if positions within the two companies were duplicative and that redundant or duplicative positions would be eliminated. Allen's analysis concluded that Harris's position was redundant, and Allen formally terminated Harris's employment. At the time Harris was terminated, six other employees were also terminated. Four of those employees were under age forty; two were over age forty.

Analysis

Direct Discrimination

The Age Discrimination in Employment Act ("ADEA") prohibits employers from firing workers who are forty or over on the basis of their age. 29 U.S.C. § 623 (2006). To prevail on a claim of age discrimination in firing, a plaintiff may show discrimination either directly or indirectly. *Fass v. Sears, Roebuck & Co.*, 532 F.3d 633, 641 (7th Cir. 2008). In either case, however, the key question is whether the plaintiff has proved intentional discrimination. *Olson v. N. FS, Inc.*, 387 F.3d 632, 635 (7th Cir. 2004).

The direct method requires a plaintiff to offer direct or circumstantial evidence that an employer's decision to terminate was motivated by age. *Tubergen v. St. Vincent Hosp. & Health Care Ctr., Inc.*, 517 F.3d 470, 473 (2d Cir. 2000). Harris has alleged that the comments by Charlton show that the decision to terminate him was motivated by age. Those comments, however, are only relevant if Charlton was either a decision maker or had singular influence over the decision maker. *See Staub v. Proctor Hosp.*, 560 F.3d 647, 651 (3d Cir. 2009). As one court has noted, "generally speaking, comments by a non-decision maker do not suffice as evidence of discriminatory intent." *Lucas v. Chi. Transit Auth.*, 367 F.3d 714, 730 (7th Cir. 2004).

In the present case, the decision maker, Allen, conducted her own analysis into the facts relevant to the decision to terminate various employment positions because they were duplicative. Thus, Charlton's comments are not relevant unless he exercised "singular influence" over Allen and used that influence to cause the adverse employment action. *See Staub*, 560 F.3d at 651. It seems highly unlikely that Charlton, a midlevel supervisor, would exert this level of influence over TechCenter's president. Thus, Harris cannot prove direct discrimination.

Indirect Discrimination

To establish a prima facie case of age discrimination under the indirect method, a plaintiff must prove all of the following: that he or she is a member of a protected class (namely, that he or she is over forty years of age); that his or her work performance met the company's legitimate expectations; that despite job performance he or she was subject to an adverse employment action; and that the company treated similarly situated employees under forty more favorably. *Fass*, 532 F.3d at 641. In any event, the ultimate burden to provide intentional discrimination always remains with the plaintiff. *Greene v. Potter*, 557 F.3d 765, 769 (8th Cir. 2009), *cert. denied*, 550 U.S. 909 (2010).

In the present case, Harris can satisfy the first element of the test (namely, that he is a member of a protected class) because he is over age forty. He will be unable to satisfy the second prong of the test because he will be unable to prove that his work performance met the company's legitimate expectations. First, the company's expectations changed after the merger when the company reasonably decided to eliminate duplicative decisions. Second, Harris's job performance had been unsatisfactory even before the merger. He was not meeting the company's legitimate expectations for its workers.

As to the third prong, it would appear that Harris was terminated both because his position was redundant and because he was an unsatisfactory performer. Thus, Harris cannot prove the third prong of a prima facie case; Harris was subject to an adverse employment action (namely, termination) *because* of his performance — not despite it.

The final issue is whether TechCenter treated similarly situated employees under forty more favorably. In the present case, of the seven employees who were terminated, four were under forty; three (including Harris) were over forty years. Harris will have an extremely difficult time proving this final prong of a prima facie case because similarly situated employees under the age of forty were not treated more favorably. In fact, more than one-half of the employees terminated were under forty. Harris cannot establish a prima facie case of age discrimination under the indirect method because he cannot prove all four elements of the test. In fact, he can only prove one element: that he is a member of a protected class.

Finally, the U.S. Supreme Court has held that in cases brought under the ADEA, it is not sufficient to show that age was a motivating factor. The plaintiff must prove that, but for his age, the adverse action would not have occurred. *Gross v. FBL Fin. Servs.*, 129 S. Ct. 2343, 2349 (2009). Although Harris may be able to show that his age possibly was a factor in the determination to terminate his employment, because his position was duplicative of others after the merger and because he had been rated as an unsatisfactory employee, his age was not a "but for" cause.

Conclusion

Harris will be highly unlikely to show that he was wrongfully terminated in violation of the ADEA because he cannot show that but for his age he would not have been terminated.

Citation Quiz. Answer the following questions using *Bluebook* rules.

1. The following citation is correct: *Jones v. Smith, supra.*   F
2. The short form *Id.* always appears with an uppercase "I."   F
3. A section symbol is always followed by a space.   T
4. The following format is correct: 11th Cir.   F
5. You must always give parallel citations for all state court cases. F
6. Pinpoint citations are needed for both quotations and   T
    paraphrases.
7. Quotations of <u>50</u> or more words should be indented.
8. Which of the following is correct:
    a. 10 U.S.C. §1244.
    b. 10 USC § 1244.
    c. 10 U.S.C. 1244 (2006).
    d. 10 U.S.C. § 1244 (2006).
9. Which of the following is correct:
    a. *Id.* at § 102.
    b. *Id.* § 102.
    c. Reynolds, *id.*
    d. *Id.* at p. 455.
10. If a book is authored by two individuals, which of the following is
    correct:
    a. John T. Fisher and Mary M. Nelson
    b. John T. Fisher, et al.
    c. John T. Fisher & Mary M. Nelson
    d. Fisher & Nelson
11. Which case name is correct:
    a. *Gregory Carson v. Jacobson Bros.*
    b. *Carson v. Jacobson Brothers*
    c. *Carson v. Jacobson Bros.*
    d. *Carson v. Jacobson*
12. Which citation is correct (assuming there are no local rules):
    a. Smith v. Jones, 901 P.2d 18, 21 (Wash. 1999).
    b. *Smith v. Jones*, 424 Wash. 2d 401, 405, 901 P.2d 18, 21 (1999).
    c. *Smith v. Jones*, 424 Wash.2d 401, 405, 901 P.2d 18, 21 (1999).
    d. *Smith v. Jones*, 901 P.2d 18, 21 (Wash. Supreme Court (1999).
13. Which citation is correct:
    a. *Phillips v. Simmons*, 48 F. Supp. 2d 901, 905-908 (S.D.N.Y. 2005).
    b. *Phillips v. Simmons*, 48 F. Supp. 2d 901, 905-08 (S.D. N.Y. 2005).

c. _Phillips v. Simmons_, 48 F. Supp. 2d 901, 905-08 (S.D.N.Y. 2005).

d. _Phillips v. Simmons_, 48 F. Supp. 2d 901, 905-08 (S. Dist. N. Y. 2005).

14. Which citation is correct when citing a treatise as a short form:

a. Moore, _supra_, at § 101.

b. Moore, _Supra_, § 101.

c. Moore, _supra_ § 101.

d. Moore, _supra_, § 101.

15. Which citation is correct:

a. _United States v. Lawson_, 450 U.S. 19, 21, 201 S. Ct. 90, 93, 89 L. Ed. 2d 430, 435 (2001).

b. _United States v. Lawson_, 450 U.S. 19, 21 (2001).

c. _U.S. v. Lawson_, 450 U.S. 19, 21 (2001).

d. _USA v. Lawson_, 450 U.S. 19, 21 (2001).

Examples of State Cases and Statutes

Notes on cases: Some of the following examples are fictitious, and examples are not given for all cases from each state. Examples marked with footnotes 1 and 3 indicate *The Bluebook* form to be used when citing a state supreme court case or state appellate court case, respectively, when local rules require parallel citations. Examples marked with footnotes 2 and 4 indicate *The Bluebook* form to be used when citing a state supreme court case or state appellate court case, respectively, in any other instance. For states that no longer publish officially, the form shown is that now used in those states. For cases decided before the date on which those states ceased official publication, follow the format of cases from other states shown in footnotes 1 and 3.

   Notes on statutes: Although parentheticals are given following the statutes (showing date and publisher, if publication is not official), most practitioners omit the parenthetical information following statutes. Examples are not given for all statutory compilations for all states. Many examples are fictitious. Note that for many states, *The Bluebook* (Table T.1) indicates a preferred format for statutes, usually citation to the official set.

   In all instances, court rules dictating citation form supersede the following forms.

Alabama*   *Employees' Benefit Ass'n v. Grissett*, 732 So. 2d 968, 972 (Ala. 1998).
                 Davis v. State, 720 So. 2d 1006, 1009 (Ala. Crim. App. 1998).
                 Alabama statute: Ala. Code § 37-2-83 (1992).

Alaska*   *Bostic v. State*, 968 P.2d 564, 566 (Alaska 1998).
                 Linton v. State, 770 P.2d 123, 126 (Alaska Ct. App. 1994).
                 Alaska statute: Alaska Stat. § 45.55.119 (1990).

Arizona   *In re Am. W. Airlines*, 179 Ariz. 528, 530, 880 P.2d 1075,
                 1777 (1998).[1] or
                    In re Am. W. Airlines, 880 P.2d 1075, 1077 (Ariz. 1998).[2]
                 Young v. Lee, 214 Ariz. App. 80, 84, 400 P.2d 103, 106
                 (1974).[3] or
                    Young v. Lee, 400 P.2d 103, 106 (Ariz. Ct. App. 1974).[5]
                 State v. Wagner, 194 Ariz. 1, 4, 976 P.2d 250, 255 (Ct.
                 App. 1998).[5]
                 Arizona statute: Ariz. Rev. Stat. Ann. § 28-7906 (1998).

Arkansas*   *Powell v. Hays*, 323 Ark. 104, 106, 3 S.W.3d 15, 18 (1995).[1] or
                    Powell v. Hays, 3 S.W.3d 15, 18 (Ark. 1995).[2]
                 Peters v. Boles, 56 Ark. App. 14, 19, 4 S.W.3d 90, 93 (1997).[3] or
                    Peters v. Boles, 4 S.W.3d 90, 93 (Ark. Ct. App. 1997).[4]
                 Gibbs v. Cox, 2010 Ark. 32, at 3, 288 S.W.3d 21, 24.[8]
                 Davis v. Davis, 2009 Ark. App. 210, at 5, 285 S.W.3d 65, 71.[8]
                 Arkansas statute: Ark. Code Ann. § 5-64-401 (1996).

California   *People v. Ortega*, 19 Cal. 4th 686, 688, 968 P.2d 48, 50, 80
                 Cal. Rptr. 489, 491 (1998).[1] or
                    People v. Ortega, 968 P.2d 48, 50 (Cal. 1998).[2]
                 Chu v. Lee, 33 Cal. App. 4th 80, 81, 229 Cal. Rptr. 6, 7
                 (1995).[3] or
                    Chu v. Lee, 229 Cal. Rptr. 6, 7 (Ct. App. 1995).
                 California statute: Cal. Educ. Code § 8403 (West 1989).
                                           Cal. Prob. Code § 1365
                                           (Deering 1991).

Colorado*   *People v. Altman*, 960 P.2d 1164, 1168 (Colo. 1998).
                 Raney v. Feist, 538 P.2d 89, 97 (Colo. App. 1990).
                 Colorado statute: Colo. Rev. Stat. § 31-10-408 (1999).
                                    Colo. Rev. Stat. Ann. § 14-10-119
                                    (West 1997).

Connecticut   *State v. Cobb*, 251 Conn. 285, 288, 743 A.2d 1, 4 (1999).[1]
                 or
                    State v. Cobb, 743 A.2d 1, 4 (Conn. 1999).[2]

Easton v. Gibb, 245 Conn. App. 14, 19, 618 A.2d 49, 54 (1987).[3] or
  Easton v. Gibb, 618 A.2d 49, 54 (Conn. App. Ct. 1987).[4]
Connecticut statute: Conn. Gen. Stat. § 29-332 (1999).
  Conn. Gen. Stat. Ann.
  § 33-687 (West 1997).

Delaware*   *DiGiacobbe v. Sestak*, 743 A.2d 180, 185 (Del. 1999).
  Rose v. Cadillac Fairview Shopping Ctr., 668 A.2d 782, 784 (Del. Ch. 1995).
  Delaware statute: Del. Code Ann. tit. 13, § 733 (1989).

District of   *Durham v. United States*, 743 A.2d 196, 199 (D.C. 1999).
Columbia*,+   District of Columbia statute: D.C. Code § 6-972 (1995).

Florida*   *DiPietro v. Griefer*, 732 So. 2d 323, 326 (Fla. 1999).
  Drury v. Jackson, 438 So. 2d 568, 571 (Fla. Dist. Ct. App. 1987).
  Florida statute: Fla. Stat. § 421.04 (1993).
  Fla. Stat. Ann. § 443.036 (West 1997).

Georgia   *Allen v. Carr*, 216 Ga. 31, 37, 489 S.E.2d 15, 21 (1993).[1] or
  Allen v. Carr, 489 S.E.2d 15, 21 (Ga. 1993).[2]
  Clay v. Park, 177 Ga. App. 22, 26, 493 S.E.2d 57, 61 (1995).[3] or
  Clay v. Park, 493 S.E.2d 57, 61 (Ga. Ct. App. 1995).[4]
  Georgia statute: Ga. Code Ann. § 49-4-149 (1998).
  Ga. Code Ann. § 38-2-93 (West 1999).

Hawaii   *State v. Maumalanga*, 90 Haw. 58, 60, 976 P.2d 372, 375 (1998).[1] or
  State v. Maumalanga, 976 P.2d 372, 375 (Haw. 1998).[2]
  Mann v. Kamalu, 89 Haw. App. 45, 47, 590 P.2d 18, 20 (1990).[3] or
  Mann v. Kamalu, 590 P.2d 18, 20 (Haw. Ct. App. 1990).[4]
  State v. Perez, 90 Haw. 113, 115, 976 P.2d 427, 430 (Ct. App. 1998).[5,7]
  Hawaii statute: Haw. Rev. Stat. § 516-32 (1997).
  Haw. Rev. Stat. Ann. § 516-62 (LexisNexis 1993).[6]

Idaho   *West v. Sonke*, 131 Idaho 133, 136, 968 P.2d 228, 231 (1998).[1] or

West v. Sonke, 968 P.2d 228, 231 (Idaho 1998).[2]
State v. Pilik, 129 Idaho 50, 53, 921 P.2d 750, 754 (Ct.
App. 1996).[3,5] or
  State v. Pilik, 921 P.2d 750, 754 (Idaho Ct. App. 1996).[4]
Idaho statute: Idaho Code Ann. § 56-805 (1994).

Illinois   *LeGout v. Decker*, 146 Ill. 2d 389, 391, 586 N.E.2d 1257,
1259, 166 Ill. Dec. 928, 931 (1992).[1] or
  LeGout v. Decker, 586 N.E.2d 1257, 1259 (Ill. 1992).[2]
Martinez v. Mobil Oil Corp., 296 Ill. App. 3d
607, 610, 694 N.E.2d 639, 641, 230 Ill. Dec. 670, 674
(1998).[3] or
  Martinez v. Mobil Oil Corp., 694 N.E.2d 639, 641 (Ill.
  App. Ct. 1998).[4]
Illinois statute: 735 Ill. Comp. Stat. 5/1-104 (1993).
                    405 Ill. Comp. Stat. Ann. 5/2-107.1
                    (West 1997).

Indiana*   *In re Edwards*, 694 N.E.2d 701, 704 (Ind. 1998).
Knaus v. York, 586 N.E.2d 909, 914 (Ind. Ct. App. 1992).
Indiana statute: Ind. Code § 28-5-1-9 (1998).
                   Ind. Code Ann. § 6-1.1-17-3
                   (West 1998).
                   Ind. Code Ann. § 28-2-16-17
                   (LexisNexis 1996).

Iowa*   *In re Wagner*, 604 N.W.2d 605, 607 (Iowa 2000).
State v. Hauan, 361 N.W.2d 336, 336 (Iowa Ct. App.
1984).
Iowa statute: Iowa Code § 422.86 (1999).
                Iowa Code Ann. § 524.106 (West 1993).

Kansas   *State v. Valentine*, 260 Kan. 431, 433, 921 P.2d 770, 773
(1996).[1] or
  State v. Valentine, 921 P.2d 770, 773 (Kan. 1996).[2]
Bryson v. Wichita State Univ., 19 Kan. App. 2d 1104,
1107, 880 P.2d 800, 804 (1994).[3] or
  Bryson v. Wichita State Univ., 880 P.2d 800, 804 (Kan.
  Ct. App. 1994).[4]
Kansas statute: Kan. Stat. Ann. § 24-621 (1993).
                  Kan. Stat. Ann. § 2-316 (West 1996).

Kentucky*	*Harrington v. Phifer*, 4 S.W.3d 918, 929 (Ky. 1995). *O'Malley v. Gonzales*, 6 S.W.3d 404, 418 (Ky. Ct. App. 1998). Kentucky statute: Ky. Rev. Stat. Ann. § 199.470 (West 1994). Ky. Rev. Stat. Ann. § 186.412 (LexisNexis 1997).
Louisiana*	*Neely v. Turner*, 720 So. 2d 673, 675 (La. 1992). *Medicus v. Scott*, 744 So. 2d 192, 195 (La. Ct. App. 1993). *Smith v. Jones*, 94-2345, p. 7 (La. 7/15/94); 650 So. 2d 500, 504.[8] *Ivey v. Simms*, 2004-1023, p. 4 (La. App. 3 Cir. 3/5/05); 780 So. 2d 122.[8] Louisiana statute: La. Rev. Stat. Ann. § 23:1142 (1998). La. Code Crim. Proc. Ann. art. 786 (1998).
Maine*,+	*D'Souza v. Garner*, 690 A.2d 671, 685 (Me. 1995). *Smith v. Jones*, 1997 ME 7, ¶ 14, 685 A.2d 110, 112.[8] Maine statute: Me. Rev. Stat. Ann. tit. 25, § 2921 (1998).

Maryland	*Save Our Sts. v. Mitchell*, 357 Md. 237, 239, 743 A.2d 748, 750 (1998).[1] or
	    Save Our Sts. v. Mitchell, 743 A.2d 748, 750 (Md. 1998).[2]
	Allied Inv. Corp. v. Jasen, 123 Md. App. 88, 90, 716 A.2d 1085, 1088 (1998).[3] or
	    Allied Inv. Corp. v. Jasen, 716 A.2d 1085, 1088 (Md. Ct. Spec. App. 1998).[4]
	Maryland statute: Md. Code Ann., Fam. Law § 7-101 (LexisNexis 1999).

Massachusetts	*In re London*, 427 Mass. 477, 479, 694 N.E.2d 337, 339 (1998).[1] or
	    In re London, 694 N.E.2d 337, 339 (Mass. 1998).[2]
	Campbell v. City Council, 32 Mass. App. Ct. 152, 155, 586 N.E.2d 1009, 1013 (1992).[3] or
	    Campbell v. City Council, 586 N.E.2d 1009, 1013 (Mass. App. Ct. 1992).[4]
	Massachusetts statute: Mass. Gen. Laws ch. 175, § 123 (1988).

	Mass. Ann. Laws ch. 183, § 30 (LexisNexis 1996).
Michigan	*Maynard v. Sauseda*, 417 Mich. 1100, 1103, 361 N.W.2d 342, 345 (1983).[1] or

Maynard v. Sauseda, 361 N.W.2d 342, 345 (Mich. 1983).[2]

Bass v. Combs, 238 Mich. App. 16, 19, 604 N.W.2d 727, 730 (1999).[3] or

Bass v. Combs, 604 N.W.2d 727, 730 (Mich. Ct. App. 1999).[4]

Michigan statute:　Mich Comp. Laws § 120.904 (1996).
　　　　　　　　　　Mich. Comp. Laws Ann.
　　　　　　　　　　§ 380.1756 (West 1997).

Minnesota*	*Knotz v. Viking Carpet*, 361 N.W.2d 872, 877 (Minn. 1985).

Boldt v. Roth, 604 N.W.2d 117, 120 (Minn. Ct. App. 2000).

Minnesota statute:　Minn. Stat. § 50.28 (1998).
　　　　　　　　　　Minn. Stat. Ann. § 541.04
　　　　　　　　　　(West 1988).

Mississippi*	*Lindsay v. State*, 720 So. 2d 182, 185 (Miss. 1996).

Ladner v. Manuel, 744 So. 2d 390, 394 (Miss. Ct. App. 1996).

Smith v. Jones, 95–KA–01234–SCT (¶ 1) (Miss. 1998).[8]

Mississippi statute:　Miss. Code Ann. § 65-11-45 (1996).

Missouri*	*Lovell v. B & H Inc.*, 909 S.W.2d 14, 18 (Mo. 1993).

Bryson v. Brant, 925 S.W.2d 689, 694 (Mo. Ct. App. 1995).

Missouri statute:　Mo. Rev. Stat. § 367.040 (1994).
　　　　　　　　　　Mo. Ann. Stat. § 534.030 (West
　　　　　　　　　　1988).

Montana+	*Horn v. Horn*, 165 Mont. 118, 129, 921 P.2d 14, 23 (1996).[1] or

Horn v. Horn, 921 P.2d 14, 23 (Mont. 1996).[2]

Dawson v. Walter, 1998 MT 12, ¶ 44, 286 Mont. 175, 968 P.2d 1312.[8]

Montana statute:　Mont. Code Ann. § 69-1-224 (1995).

Nebraska	*State v. Nebraska*, 258 Neb. 511, 513, 604 N.W.2d 151, 154 (2000).[1] or

State v. Nebraska, 604 N.W.2d 151, 154 (Neb. 2000).[2]
Reinsch v. Reinsch, 8 Neb. App. 852, 854, 602 N.W.2d 261, 264 (1999).[3] or
   Reinsch v. Reinsch, 602 N.W.2d 261, 264 (Neb. Ct. App. 1999).[4]
Nebraska statute: Neb. Rev. Stat. § 72-221 (1996).
                     Neb. Rev. Stat. Ann. § 54-101 (LexisNexis 1995).

Nevada[+]   *Shaw v. Gammon*, 113 Nev. 24, 29, 960 P.2d 18, 23 (1998).[1] or
   Shaw v. Gammon, 960 P.2d 18, 23 (Nev. 1998).[2]
Nevada statute: Nev. Rev. Stat. § 243.490 (1999).
                 Nev. Rev. Stat. Ann. § 319.350 (LexisNexis 1999).

New Hampshire[+] *Moore v. Tyler*, 89 N.H. 114, 118, 743 A.2d 681, 686 (1999).[1] or
   Moore v. Tyler, 743 A.2d 681, 686 (N.H. 1999).[2]
New Hampshire statute: N.H. Rev. Stat. Ann. § 391:7 (1998).

New Jersey   *Roach v. TRW, Inc.*, 162 N.J. 195, 197, 743 A.2d 847, 850 (1999).[1] or
   Roach v. TRW, Inc., 743 A.2d 847, 850 (N.J. 1999).[2]
Bell v. Bell, 312 N.J. Super. 13, 15, 716 A.2d 318, 321 (1998).[3] or
   Bell v. Bell, 716 A.2d 318, 321 (N.J. Super. Ct. App. Div. 1998).[4]
New Jersey statute: N.J. Stat. Ann. § 17:48-6 (West 1996).

New Mexico   *Barone v. Torres*, 127 N.M. 20, 23, 976 P.2d 21, 24 (1994).[1] or
   Barone v. Torres, 976 P.2d 21, 24 (N.M. 1994).[2]
State v. Ray, 1998-NMSC-009, ¶ 4, 122 N.M. 23, 909 P.2d 112.[8]
Key v. Chrysler Motors Corp., 127 N.M. 98, 99, 996 P.2d 523, 524 (Ct. App. 1994).[3,5] or
   Key v. Chrysler Motors Corp., 996 P.2d 523, 524 (N.M. Ct. App. 1994).[4]
Nelson v. Lee, 2000-NMCA-109, ¶ 11, 128 N.M. 14, 972 P.2d 111.[8]
New Mexico statute: N.M. Stat. Ann. § 31-2-3 (1997).

New York

Furch v. Bacci, 91 N.Y.2d 953, 955, 694 N.E.2d 880, 882, 666 N.Y.S.2d 300, 302 (1998).[1] or
 Furch v. Bacci, 694 N.E.2d 880, 882 (N.Y. 1998).[2]
Pryce v. Fowell, 257 A.D.2d 275, 277, 594 N.Y.S.2d 82, 84 (1997).[3] or
 Pryce v. Fowell, 594 N.Y.S.2d 82, 84 (App. Div. 1997).[4]
Macy v. Frye, 108 Misc. 2d 994, 997, 438 N.Y.S.2d 156, 160 (Sup. Ct. 1980).[3] or
 Macy v. Frye, 438 N.Y.S.2d 156, 160 (Sup. Ct. 1980).[4]
New York statute: N.Y. Dom. Rel. Law § 23 (McKinney 1999).
       N.Y. Gen. Bus. Law § 353 (Consol. 1999).

North Carolina

O'Brien v. Matthews, 280 N.C. 42, 47, 185 S.E.2d 123, 126 (1975).[1] or
 O'Brien v. Matthews, 185 S.E.2d 123, 126 (N.C. 1975).[2]
Mill v. Lodge, 5 N.C. App. 657, 659, 169 S.E.2d 36, 39 (1969).[3] or
 Mill v. Lodge, 169 S.E.2d 36, 39 (N.C. Ct. App. 1969).[4]
North Carolina statute: N.C. Gen. Stat. § 34-2 (1999).
        N.C. Gen. Stat. Ann. § 105-33 (West 1999).

North Dakota*

Lyon v. Ford Motor Co., 604 N.W.2d 453, 455 (N.D. 1996).
Fabricut, Inc. v. Keeney, 429 N.W.2d 24, 29 (N.D. Ct. App. 1988).
Adams v. North, 1999 ND 32, ¶ 4, 600 N.W.2d 91, 95.[8]
North Dakota statute: N.D. Cent. Code § 28-01-18 (1996).

Ohio

Columbus Bar Ass'n v. Dye, 82 Ohio St. 3d 64, 67, 694 N.E.2d 440, 443 (1998).[1] or
 Columbus Bar Ass'n v. Dye, 694 N.E.2d 440, 443 (Ohio 1998).[2]
Brown v. Dana, 66 Ohio App. 3d 709, 711, 586 N.E.2d 150, 153 (1990).[3] or
 Brown v. Dana, 586 N.E.2d 150, 153 (Ohio Ct. App. 1990).[4]
State v. Harris, 99 Ohio St. 3d 29, 2003-Ohio-1189, 791 N.E.2d 22, at ¶ 14.[8]

Ohio statute:	Ohio Rev. Code Ann. § 4507.3 (LexisNexis 1999). Ohio Rev. Code Ann. § 101.5 (West 1999).

Oklahoma*

Nation v. State Farm Ins. Co., 880 P.2d 877, 890 (Okla. 1994).

Peterson v. Baker, 921 P.2d 955, 963 (Okla. Civ. App. 1996).

Skelly v. State, 880 P.2d 401, 405 (Okla. Crim. App. 1994).

Gray v. Carey, 1999 OK 44, ¶ 4, 978 P.2d 490, 494.[8]

Oklahoma statute: Okla. Stat. tit. 73, § 83.2 (1991). Okla. Stat. Ann. tit. 68, § 1353 (West 1992).

Oregon

Tellam v. Birch, 321 Or. 1, 3, 921 P.2d 380, 384 (1996).[1] or
  Tellam v. Birch, 921 P.2d 380, 384 (Or. 1996).[2]

Enders v. Enders, 154 Or. App. 142, 144, 960 P.2d 986, 989 (1997).[3] or
  Enders v. Enders, 960 P.2d 986, 989 (Or. Ct. App. 1997).[4]

Oregon statute: Or. Rev. Stat. § 576.175 (1997). Or. Rev. Stat. Ann. § 657A.290 (West 1994).

Pennsylvania

Cope v. Miller, 389 Pa. 116, 119, 716 A.2d 18, 22 (1998).[1] or
  Cope v. Miller, 716 A.2d 18, 22 (Pa. 1998).[2]

Hardy v. Sells, 422 Pa. Super. 4, 9, 639 A.2d 909, 914 (1993).[3] or
  Hardy v. Sells, 639 A.2d 909, 914 (Pa. Super. Ct. 1993).[4]

Bosworth v. Diaz, 691 A.2d 47, 52 (Pa. Commw. Ct. 1999).

Peters v. Cope, 2000 PA Super 111.[8]

Pennsylvania statute: 23 Pa. Cons. Stat. § 5303 (1997). 15 Pa. Cons. Stat. Ann. § 224 (West 1996).

Rhode Island*,[+]

Estrada v. Walker, 743 A.2d 1026, 1034 (R.I. 1999).

Rhode Island statute: R.I. Gen. Laws § 42-64-9 (1998).

South Carolina

Sullivan v. Pine, 331 S.C. 190, 199, 502 S.E.2d 19, 29 (1998).[1] or

Sullivan v. Pine, 502 S.E.2d 19, 29 (S.C. 1998).[2]
McKee v. Hall, 331 S.C. 560, 566, 500 S.E.2d 909, 914 (Ct. App. 1993).[3,5] or
  McKee v. Hall, 500 S.E.2d 909, 914 (S.C. Ct. App. 1993).[4]
South Carolina statute: S.C. Code Ann. § 44-7-220 (1985).

South Dakota[*,+] *Meinders v. Weber*, 604 N.W.2d 148, 150 (S.D. 1995).
Hoogestraat v. Barnett, 1998 SD 104, ¶ 5, 595 N.W.2d 900, 904.[8]
South Dakota statute: S.D. Codified Laws § 29A-2-21 (1997).

Tennessee[*] *Booker v. Allen*, 931 S.W.2d 970, 977 (Tenn. 1993).
Davis v. Crane, 918 S.W.2d 887, 892 (Tenn. Ct. App. 1987).
State v. Doyle, 920 S.W.2d 101, 104 (Tenn. Crim. App. 1989).
Tennessee statute: Tenn. Code Ann. § 17-1-304 (1994).

Texas[*] *Kroger Co. v. Robins*, 5 S.W.3d 221, 224 (Tex. 1999).
Peterson v. Reyna, 920 S.W.2d 285, 288 (Tex. Crim. App. 1994).
Allen v. Esterly, 921 S.W.2d 104, 109 (Tex. App. 1995).
Texas statute: Tex. Educ. Code Ann. § 102.12 (West 1991).

Utah[*] *Salt Lake City v. Smoot*, 921 P.2d 1003, 1005 (Utah 1996).
Gregory v. Hendrix, 880 P.2d 18, 24 (Utah Ct. App. 1994).
Allen v. Ray, 1999 UT 240, ¶ 4, 16 P.3d 1.[8]
Wiley v. Edwards, 2003 UT App 130, ¶ 9, 24 P.3d 56.
Utah statute: Utah Code Ann. § 39-6-37 (LexisNexis 1998).

Vermont[+] *Winn v. Riley*, 161 Vt. 16, 24, 743 A.2d 209, 214 (1999).[1] or
  Winn v. Riley, 743 A.2d 209, 214 (Vt. 1994).[2]
Talbot v. Dowd, 2004 VT 111, ¶ 4, 171 Vt. 104, 108, 749 A.2d 406, 409.
Vermont statute: Vt. Stat. Ann. tit. 24, § 1312 (1992).

Virginia *Sheldon v. Drye*, 225 Va. 11, 19, 445 S.E.2d 89, 94 (1995).[1] or
  Sheldon v. Drye, 445 S.E.2d 89, 94 (Va. 1995).[2]
Ruiz v. Harley, 25 Va. App. 16, 20, 486 S.E.2d 90, 95 (1997).[3] or

　　　　　　　　　Ruiz v. Harley, 486 S.E.2d 90, 95 (Va. Ct. App. 1997).[4]
　　　　　　　　　Virginia statute:　Va. Code Ann. § 33.1-226 (1996).

Washington　　　*Brewer v. Brewer*, 137 Wash. 2d 756, 758, 976 P.2d 102,
　　　　　　　　　104 (1999).[1] or
　　　　　　　　　　Brewer v. Brewer, 976 P.2d 102, 104 (Wash. 1999).[2]
　　　　　　　　　State v. Hunt, 75 Wash. App. 795, 797, 880 P.2d 96, 99
　　　　　　　　　(1994).[3] or
　　　　　　　　　　State v. Hunt, 880 P.2d 96, 99 (Wash. Ct. App. 1994).[4]
　　　　　　　　　Washington statute:　Wash. Rev. Code § 80.36.310
　　　　　　　　　　　　　　　　　　　(1998).
　　　　　　　　　　　　　　　　　　　Wash. Rev. Code Ann.
　　　　　　　　　　　　　　　　　　　§ 35.21.403 (West 1990).

West Virginia[+]　*Farrel v. Bond*, 156 W. Va. 450, 456, 295 S.E.2d 19, 25
　　　　　　　　　(1973).[1] or
　　　　　　　　　　Farrel v. Bond, 295 S.E.2d 19, 25 (W. Va. 1973).[2]
　　　　　　　　　West Virginia statute:　W. Va. Code § 17A-4-5 (1996).
　　　　　　　　　　　　　　　　　　　W. Va. Code Ann. § 19-104
　　　　　　　　　　　　　　　　　　　(LexisNexis 19xx).

Wisconsin　　　　*In re Parsons*, 122 Wis. 2d 186, 188, 361 N.W.2d 687, 690
　　　　　　　　　(1985).[1] or
　　　　　　　　　　In re Parsons, 361 N.W.2d 687, 690 (Wis. 1985).[2]
　　　　　　　　　Smith v. Jones, 2000 WI 14, ¶ 6, 240 Wis. 2d 220, 650
　　　　　　　　　N.W.2d 17.[8]
　　　　　　　　　State v. Schultz, 145 Wis. 2d 661, 663, 429 N.W.2d 79, 81
　　　　　　　　　(Ct. App. 1988).[3,5] or
　　　　　　　　　　State v. Schultz, 429 N.W.2d 79, 81 (Wis. Ct. App.
　　　　　　　　　1988).[4]
　　　　　　　　　Doe v. Roe, 2000 WI App 346, ¶ 27, 239 Wis. 2d 14, 648
　　　　　　　　　N.W.2d 81.[8]
　　　　　　　　　Wisconsin statute:　Wis. Stat. § 480.08 (1996).
　　　　　　　　　　　　　　　　　　　Wis. Stat. Ann. § 70.22
　　　　　　　　　　　　　　　　　　　(West 1999).

Wyoming[*,+]　　　*Ruwart v. Wagner*, 880 P.2d 586, 590 (Wyo. 1994).
　　　　　　　　　Allen v. Eddy, 2005 WY 10, ¶ 6, 81 P.3d 107, 114 (Wyo.
　　　　　　　　　2005).[8]
　　　　　　　　　Wyoming statute:　Wyo. Stat. Ann. § 39-16-210 (1999).

[*]State no longer publishes officially.

[+]State has no intermediate appellate courts.

[1]Case from supreme court of the state being cited in a document when court rules require parallel citations.

[2]Case from state supreme court being cited in a document that does not require parallel citations.

[3]Case from state intermediate court being cited in a document when court rules require parallel citations.

[4]Case from state intermediate court being cited in a document that does not require parallel citations.

[5]Appellate court cases are published in same volumes as supreme court cases; thus, parenthetical information is needed to identify the court that decided the case.

[6]LexisNexis has begun publishing a number of state statutes.

[7]Beginning in 1994, Hawaii appellate court cases are also published in West's *Hawaii Reports.*

[8]Vendor-neutral or public domain citation form.

Index

A

ABA Legal Technology Resource
Center, Uniform Citation
Standards, 28
Abbreviations in case names, 19–20, 78
Administrative decisions, 65–66
Administrative materials:
administrative decisions, 65–66
agency law, 63–64
presidential and executive materials, 67
rules and regulations, 64
Treasury regulations, 65
Agency law, 63–64
Alabama, 23, 25, 27, 30, 145
Alaska, 23, 27, 30, 146
Alphabetizing, 107
A.L.R. Annotations, 60–61
Alterations, 84–85
American Association of Law Libraries
(AALL), 27, 28
American Bar Association (ABA), 27
American Jurisprudence, 59
American Law Reports, 60–61
Arizona, 23, 25, 30, 146
Arkansas, 23, 27, 28, 29, 30, 146
Asking for help, 7
At, use of, 93
Atlantic Reporter, 23
Authenticated documents, 70

B

Bills, 50
Bluebook, 1, 2–3, 5
administrative materials
Rule 14, Table T1.2, 63–67
A.L.R. Annotations
Rule 16.7.6, 60–61
alterations
Rule 5.2, 84–85
books and treatises
Rule 15; B8, 57–58
capitalization
Rule 8; B7.3, 99–101

case names
abbreviations in, 19–20
Rule 10.2; B4.1.1, 18–20
constitutions
Rule 11; B6, 53
court rules
Rule 12.9.3; B5.1.3, 52
dictionaries
Rule 15.8; B8, 59
encyclopedias
Rule 15.8; B8.1, 59–60
federal court cases B4.1.3; Table T.1,
29–35
history of, 3–4
internal cross-references
Rule 3.5, 93–94, 110
Internet
Rule 18, 69–71
legislative materials
bills, 50
committee hearings, 51
committee reports, 51
floor debates, 51–52
Rule 13; B5.1.6, 50–52
omissions
Rule 5.3, 83–84
organization of, 4
parentheticals
Rule 1.5; 10.6; 10.7; B4.1.5; B11, 85–86
periodical materials
Rule 16; B9, 58–59
public domain citations
Rules 10.3.3; Table T1.3, 27–29
punctuation
Rule 1.1; 1.4; B2, 77–78
quotations
Rule 5; B4.1.2; B12, 79–83
record materials
Rule 10.8.3; B7; BT.1, 72–73
related authority
Rule 1.6, 99
Restatements
Rule 12.9.5; B5.1.3, 60

159